PUFFIN CANAL

WHISPERS FROM THE CAMPS

KATHY KACER is the author of ten books of historical fiction and non-fiction for young people that deal with the Holocaust. She has won many awards for her writing, including the Silver Birch, the Red Maple, the Hackmatack, and the Jewish Book Award. Kathy lives in Toronto with her husband and two children, and travels around the country speaking about the importance of understanding the Holocaust and keeping its memory alive.

SHARON E. McKAY has been an author for more than twenty years and in the process has written more than twenty-two fiction and non-fiction books. Her list of award wins and nominations include the Bilson Award, the IODE, the UNESCO International Youth Library, Europe's White Raven Award, and Canada's Governor General's Award.

WHISPERS
from the
CAMPS

KATHY KACER

AND

SHARON E. McKAY

PUFFIN
CANADA

PUFFIN CANADA

Published by the Penguin Group

Penguin Group (Canada), 90 Eglinton Avenue East, Suite 700,
Toronto, Ontario, Canada M4P 2Y3 (a division of Pearson Canada Inc.)

Penguin Group (USA) Inc., 375 Hudson Street, New York, New York 10014, U.S.A.
Penguin Books Ltd, 80 Strand, London WC2R 0RL, England
Penguin Ireland, 25 St Stephen's Green, Dublin 2, Ireland
(a division of Penguin Books Ltd)
Penguin Group (Australia), 250 Camberwell Road, Camberwell, Victoria 3124,
Australia (a division of Pearson Australia Group Pty Ltd)
Penguin Books India Pvt Ltd, 11 Community Centre, Panchsheel Park,
New Delhi – 110 017, India
Penguin Group (NZ), 67 Apollo Drive, Rosedale, North Shore 0745, Auckland,
New Zealand (a division of Pearson New Zealand Ltd)
Penguin Books (South Africa) (Pty) Ltd, 24 Sturdee Avenue, Rosebank,
Johannesburg 2196, South Africa

Penguin Books Ltd, Registered Offices: 80 Strand, London WC2R 0RL, England

First published 2009

1 2 3 4 5 6 7 8 9 10

Manufactured in Canada.

ISBN: 978-0-14-331252-9

Library and Archives Canada Cataloguing in Publication data
available upon request to the publisher.

Visit the Penguin Group (Canada) website at **www.penguin.ca**

Special and corporate bulk purchase rates available; please see
www.penguin.ca/corporatesales or call 1-800-810-3104, ext. 477 or 474

"*I simply can't build my hopes on a foundation of confusion, misery and death ... I think peace and tranquility will return again.*"

ANNE FRANK

CONTENTS

CONTENTS

INTRODUCTION

THIS BOOK IS MADE UP of bits of stories that together make a bigger story. They are all true, and everyone lived to tell their tales. So how do small pieces of a story taken from different lives come together and give us that big picture? Imagine an apartment building five, six storeys high. Now imagine chopping it in half and opening it up—rather like opening up a child's dollhouse. Look into all the different apartments. Press your ear up against the walls and hear the whispers; listen, imagine.

The Holocaust was the murder of more than six million Jewish people by the German Nazis, and their collaborators, during the Second World War. Under the leadership of Adolf Hitler, the Nazis didn't murder only Jews. They also killed the Roma people (once known as Gypsies), homosexuals, children and adults who were physically or mentally handicapped, millions of Poles and Russians, and anyone else who did not fit with the Nazis' view of a perfect race. *But the Jews of Europe were the only group that the Nazis deliberately intended to wipe off the face of the earth.* And since the Nazis believed that they would eventually conquer Britain and win the war, plans were in the works to kill not only every Jewish person in Europe, but those in England, Scotland, and Ireland as well.

Most of the murders of Jewish people took place during the Second World War, from 1939 to 1945, but the majority of historians suggest that the war against the Jews actually began in 1933, when Adolf Hitler first came to power in Germany. Almost immediately, he began to introduce laws and rules that targeted Jewish people for discrimination. It was also in 1933 that the first concentration camp was built, in Dachau, Germany. This camp was not built specifically to imprison Jews. In fact, the first people to occupy the camp were Communists, teachers, professors, and other people who did not agree with the Nazi agenda.

The term "concentration camp" is generally used to describe all of the Nazi prison camps, but in fact, there were several different types of camps. There were labour camps, transit camps, prisoner-of-war camps, and, of course, the death camps, the most infamous being Auschwitz. There were also many small camps that were built right beside factories, where Jewish prisoners were made to work under terrible conditions. In total, there were more than a hundred major concentration camps, and thousands of smaller ones. As the war progressed, the distinctions between these camps became more blurred as more and more people were being killed inside. Living conditions in all of the camps were brutal and inhumane. Many died there from cruel treatment, harsh working conditions, malnutrition, and overcrowding.

Here's how Alex Feuer, then only fifteen years old, described his arrival at the Auschwitz concentration camp.

At the ripe old age of fifteen I arrived in Auschwitz, the infamous human extermination camp. We were pushed like cattle into freight train cars. After a five-day, unbelievable hard journey, we arrived in Auschwitz. As we were being removed from the train, our first view was SS men with guns and guard dogs. The SS guards told us to leave the little belongings we had on the ground and line up. Little did we know at the time that we were about to be selected for life or for death. As I stood in line a stranger tapped me on the shoulders from behind and told me in Yiddish: "Little boy, stand on your feet. Stand on your toes when you come up to the German SS. Make yourself taller." I stretched and strained, somehow knowing that my life depended upon the stranger's advice.[1]

The development of the concentration camps can be divided into three time periods. From 1933 to 1936, the

---

[1] Yad Vashem Archives O.3-8521, "From the Testimony of Alex Feuer about the Arrival and First Selection at Auschwitz."

camps were constructed to imprison political opponents to Adolf Hitler and his Nazi Party. From 1936 to 1942, most of the camps that were constructed were hard-labour camps. The death camps were established between 1942 and 1945.

By the end of 1941, Hitler had devised a plan to kill all the Jewish people of Europe. He called this plan "The Final Solution." It didn't matter to Hitler if you were young or old, rich or poor, educated or unschooled. If you were Jewish, you were targeted for deportation to the camps. Six death camps were constructed in Poland for the purpose of carrying out Hitler's plan: Auschwitz-Birkenau, Treblinka, Belzec, Sobibor, Majdanek, and Chelmno. The primary purpose of these camps was to kill as many Jews as possible, as quickly as possible, by gassing, shooting, and other means.

While most of the ghettos were constructed in the middle of a city or right beside train lines, and therefore in plain sight, attempts were made to conceal the true nature of the concentration camps. All the death camps were built in far-flung areas of Poland. While the German Nazis made some attempt to cover their tracks, the murder of millions was undertaken not in a frenzy of irrational anger, but in a deliberate, thought-out process. Hundreds of thousands were involved in the construction of ghettos and camps, roads and railway lines. The slaughter of this many people could not have happened without the co-operation of the local police and the indifference of the populations living in the different countries conquered by the Third Reich.

By the end of the Second World War, six million Jewish people had perished, the majority of them in the death camps of Poland. One and a half million of those were children. They died horrible, cruel, and often lonely deaths. Only with the defeat of Nazi Germany by the Allied Forces did the Holocaust come to an end, in 1945.

All of the people you will meet between these covers survived, and while all carry scars, all have carved out rich and useful lives.

Read with your heart. Listen to the whispers.

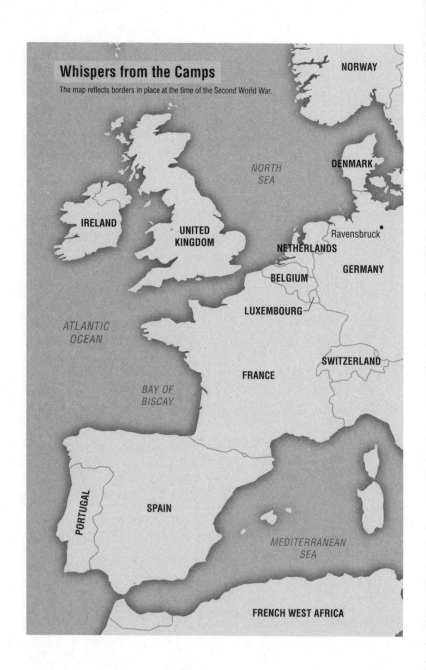

Whispers from the Camps

The map reflects borders in place at the time of the Second World War.

NORWAY

DENMARK

NORTH
SEA

IRELAND

UNITED
KINGDOM

Ravensbruck

NETHERLANDS

GERMANY

BELGIUM

LUXEMBOURG

ATLANTIC
OCEAN

SWITZERLAND

FRANCE

BAY OF
BISCAY

PORTUGAL

SPAIN

MEDITERRANEAN
SEA

FRENCH WEST AFRICA

THE FUNERAL PARADE

Felicia, five years old, in Vatra Dornei, Romania.

"DEAD," pronounced Felicia. "It's a corpse."

"It's a dead corpse," David, her not-really-best-friend-because-he-could-be-annoying, readily agreed. Just to make very sure it was dead he nudged the bird with his shoe. "What shall we do with it?"

Felicia—or Fella, for short—bent down to take a closer look. "We should have a funeral."

"It should be a big funeral," said David.

"Very big."

Neither ten-year-old Fella nor eight-year-old David had ever actually been to a funeral, but they had seen pictures of a funeral procession in the newspaper. They were wonderful things: horse-drawn coaches, coffins behind glass, people dressed in black following behind, fine ladies wearing long, flowing veils and sniffing into white lace hankies—like a parade! Of course the picture in the paper was of a royal funeral, but why shouldn't a dead bird have a royal funeral?

"I'll get a coffin. You go and tell everyone to come," said Fella, who was not only older but bossier too. "We'll have a funeral parade!"

"A dead-bird funeral parade!" yelled David over his shoulder as he ran off to gather some mourners.

There would be plenty of children about. It was 1941, and the Jewish children of Romania were no longer allowed to go to school. David thought that that was a good thing, but Fella wasn't so sure. She had always liked school. But when she thought about it, it hadn't been the same lately. Some of the teachers had been mean. Before all the Jewish children were banned from classrooms, her teacher had called her up to the front of the class and said that she would never grow any taller than she was now ... because she was Jewish. Then the teacher had hit her on the head with the black, leather-bound attendance book. Almost all the teachers had picked on the Jewish children then.

Fella climbed the steps up to her family's apartment. Grandfather and Grandmother had built the house, then divided it into private quarters. Her grandparents lived downstairs, and Fella lived with her parents upstairs. Their home was big and spacious, and Fella had her own room. A long veranda ran the whole length of the house on both floors.

From the veranda, Fella could see the hills, the mountains, the tall evergreen trees, and the Dorna River too. There was a veil of mist across the mountains today. Soon it would be winter, and people from all around would come to ski. Then summer would come, and tourists would return for the mineral waters and mud baths. And everyone came all through the year to go to the casino. Ladies in long dresses and men in tuxedos—it was all wonderful. Not that Fella had ever been inside the casino, and really, she had never actually seen these fine ladies and gentlemen in their fancy evening clothes, since she was in bed by then, but she had seen pictures, and she could imagine.

"Fella, is that you?" Mama called from the kitchen.

Fella stopped short and drew in a breath. What day was it? Mama did the white wash on Mondays and the coloured wash on Tuesdays. Today was Wednesday—cleaning day. It was sometimes hard remembering the days of the week when there wasn't school to go to. Of course it was cleaning day. Look—the carpets were already hanging over the railings waiting to be beaten. Mama cleaned all the time. Everything in the house had to shine—even Fella!

"Fella, what are you up to?"

Fella looked down at her white socks and black patent-leather shoes. Her shoes were dusty. "Nothing, Mama, nothing." She made a dash for the attic.

Tata, Fella's father, owned a store in the middle of town. Sometimes he brought home old shoeboxes from the store and used them to store things in the attic. A shoebox would make a perfect bird coffin. Fella nabbed a box and ran.

In no time she was back outside, and the dead bird was safely laid to rest in the shoebox. Just as the deed was done, David returned with the mourners. Fella organized the gaggle of children, clasped the shoebox in her hands, and the funeral march through town began.

"We should sing," suggested Rebecca. She was eleven.

"No, we are supposed to be silent. Only Christians sing at funerals," said Marcel, who was twelve.

None of the ten children who had gathered had been to either a Christian or Jewish funeral, and so they all had equal expertise. More children were joining the parade by the minute, and it was decided that they should progress through the town solemnly. And so, two by two, and then three by three, they went through the town in silence.

Fella paused at the park entrance. The park was Fella's favourite place. The gazebo in the middle had a grey tin dome on the top, rather like a funny hat, and beautiful wooden latticework around the small arches. In summer, bands would play in the gazebo, and Mama and Tata would take her for long walks to see the flowers, buy ice cream, and sit on the benches. Music was everywhere; it seemed to float up and up, into the mountains. That was before they were told that Jews were not allowed to sit on benches. Jews were not even supposed to go into the park! Jews weren't allowed to do a lot of things now.

It wasn't fair that Jewish children were not allowed to go into the park. Fella and her friends wouldn't hurt anything. They would stay on the paths and not tramp across the flower beds. It just wasn't fair, and if she met one of those mean Iron Guard fascist soldiers she would tell him that too. The Iron Guards were Romanian soldiers, but they were just as awful as those Nazi soldiers, and they did everything the Nazis said, anyway.

Fella made a decision and led the line of mourners through the park entrance and past the medieval tower, with its grey stone steps and turrets, that surrounded the mineral water well. Tata used to collect water from the well. It was kept in their icebox. It was delicious. On the children marched, past the flower beds and the lovely manicured lawns towards the gazebo.

"David, what are you doing?" Fella stopped short so quickly that Sonia, Eva, and Laura banged into her, and

Fredy and Persi bumped into them. David was kneeling in front of a squirrel. The squirrels were so tame that they would come right up to people and eat nuts from an open palm. But David didn't have any nuts. The squirrel sniffed at David's hands, then looked around, confused. "David, stop it. That's teasing," fumed Fella. David grinned, shrugged, and the parade continued out of the park and into the town.

"Look!" It was little Eva who spotted the Iron Guards. "Run!" The entire parade bolted out of the far gate. The guards paid them no mind at all.

Once outside the gate, the mourners marched towards the centre of the town. Most of the Jewish families in Vatra Dornei lived there. They were doctors, dentists, lawyers, shop owners, bakers, barbers, tailors, and shoemakers too. Tata's store was there too. The great town hall sat in the middle of the town. It was there, on the stone steps, that announcements were made. They heard a drum roll.

"Hurry up!" shouted a child. The children surged forward. Fella and David picked up the pace too.

Before the war, before Hitler had come to power in the country called Germany, it had been fun to hear the news read out loud at the town hall. It wasn't fun any more. Now, a boy who belonged to the Iron Guards stood beside the drummer on the stone steps. It was his job to read out new rules, and sometimes add silly twists to old rules. He would start with, "Jews must wear a yellow star on their clothing."

A few days later he would say, "Jews must wear a yellow star *with black piping around it.*" Then, "Jews must wear a yellow star *on top of a black background.*" There were lots and lots more rules—when to shop, when to walk on the street, when to go out, and when to stay inside. Then there were lists of punishments for those who did not obey the new rules. All these rules upset the adults terribly.

A lot of people had turned out to hear the announcements today. Fella strained, then stood on tippy-toes. Tata would be in the crowd around the steps of the town hall. Her uncle would likely be there, too, and most of the Jewish men and some of the women in the town. It was no use, she couldn't see him.

"Let's not go too close," said Fella, and all the mourners agreed.

The children marched—two by two, three by three—past their beautiful synagogue. It was all closed up now. Fella remembered that something bad had happened at the synagogue a few weeks before. All the Jewish men had been locked up in it, and the soldiers had said they would burn it down unless they were given lots of money. The men were left in there for three days without any food or water. Fella turned away with a shudder.

Fella could see her house once again, and beyond the house was the Dorna River. It was so pretty that it was easy to forget the Iron Guards and all the silly rules. Tata said that it would all be over soon and everything would go back to the way it was, and Fella believed him.

"Fella." David nudged her, then looked at the dead-bird coffin. It was time for the funeral.

By now there were thirty children gathered in Fella's backyard. All stood silently, hands folded, around the grave David had hastily dug—a little hole under a little tree. Slowly and reverently, the shoebox was lowered into the ground. A prayer of sorts was muttered, dirt shifted over the shoebox, and finally a rock was placed over top. David dropped it with a *thunk*. And then it began to rain.

"Fella, come into the house. Children, go home to your parents," Tata called down from the veranda. What a funny thing! And he sounded funny too—not angry, just odd! And why was he home for his midday meal so very early?

No one said goodbye, no one said anything, the children just scattered in different directions as Fella raced up the stairs, two at a time, and barged into the apartment. Oh, her shoes were muddy! Mama would be angry. Then another funny thing happened—Mama didn't notice the mud on her floor or on the shoes! Mama was pacing up and down and shaking her head this way and that as Tata thumped down hard on a chair. What was wrong?

"Where are we to go? Take food for three days—will we be home in three days? Where will they take us? We must lock up the house and the store. And one suitcase each? How long can a person live out of one suitcase? What does this mean?" Poor Mama was talking and moving about in circles. Tata's face was ashen.

"Tata, what's happened?" Fella touched her father's sleeve. Poor Tata, he was always worried.

"We are going on a trip, Fella, by train," said Tata gently.

"Is everyone going, Tata?" Fella asked.

"Only the Jews, dear girl," Tata added in a low, sombre voice. "Now go, help your mama pack. We must be at the train station at five o'clock. I will see to the store."

But when Tata left, Mama did not pack the suitcases. Instead she cleaned the house.

"Help me, Fella."

Mama handed Fella a broom. The house was already spotless, anyone could see that.

Mama, I'm scared. Mama, why are you cleaning? Fella wanted to ask, but instead Fella swept the clean floor.

With a hastily packed knapsack on her back and padded with three layers of clothes, Fella, her parents, grandparents, Auntie Mila, and Uncle Armin waited for the train promptly at five o'clock. Fella strained to see who was at the train station. There were so many people. Her friends had to be around somewhere, but she couldn't see them, it was too crowded. Mama and Tata would not let her leave their side to go and look. Why were so many people travelling at the same time?

The light rain continued. Oh, she was *so* damp and chilly. When would the train come? A big passenger train raced into the station and stopped. Was this their train? Why were the soldiers keeping people from getting on? She could see inside. The train was filled with people sitting on soft, velvet seats, or long, wooden benches. There was a conductor, too, in a nice suit. Maybe there would be a conductor on their train, and maybe he would pass out sandwiches. Fella waved but the people turned away. Then a second train came and the same thing happened.

Six o'clock came and went, then seven, eight, nine. She didn't wave any more. It was hard to stand and wait in the rain. She wasn't chilly any more, either, she was cold. Babies cried and sick people moaned. Little children wanted their supper. She could hear people talking. What of the pets left behind? Who would feed the puppy, the budgie, the cat? Everyone was wet, cold, tired, and worried.

"Look, Tata." Fella pointed into the dark. Finally, they could see the headlight of a very long train in the distance. It drew closer and closer. They could hear the thin screech of the train's brakes. It was stopping. No, this could not be their train. It was for animals, cows maybe. The train stopped and doors as big as walls slid open. Something smelled bad. There was an awful stink coming from inside the train. Fella covered her nose.

"*Repede!*" yelled a Legionnaire, a soldier, who jumped off

the train. He pointed his rifle right at them! *"REPEDE!* Hurry!"

Why was he yelling? Why was he so mean? Why did they have to hurry? They had been waiting for hours and hours. It wasn't their fault that the train was late. But then everyone seemed to move at once. They surged forward. The younger men and boys jumped up into the cars first and turned to help others climb up, but something was wrong. Once people were on board, they all slid and slipped, like they were on ice. The soldiers were yelling bad words. Why did they keep on yelling?

"Come, Fella." Papa picked her up and pushed her into the car. One foot slid out from under her. The floor was covered in hay and fresh manure—that was why it smelled so bad. That was why everyone was slipping around. All the floors of the cattle cars were covered in cow poop. Didn't they have time to clean it? Why were they travelling in a train with cow poop? And where were the benches? And where was the toilet? Where was the conductor?

More and more people piled in behind her. She couldn't breathe. "Tata? Mama?" Fella cried out. Oh, she was being crushed! *Ow,* an elbow clipped her ear. The car was full and they were still shoving people in.

"Tata? Mama?"

"We're here, Fella," Mama cried back.

Fella couldn't reach her through the crowd of people. "Mama, Mama," cried Fella. "Mama, help me!"

Someone closed the door, maybe one of the soldiers. A bolt was drawn. They were locked in!

"Mama, Tata, I can't see anything!" Darkness—it was like falling down a well or being shut in a dungeon. Everything went black.

POSTSCRIPT

That morning, Felicia Steigman Carmelly had been a little girl doing little-girl things in her familiar, safe town. Hours later, she'd been plunged into what we now know as the twentieth century's darkest hour. Felicia would suffer through horrendous experiences in the concentration camp and see the deaths of many of her extended family members.

The camp that Felicia and her family were sent to was in Transnistria, a name coined by the Germans at the beginning of the Second World War. Most of it is now an independent republic bordering Moldova. Transnistria was liberated by the Soviet armies in the spring of 1944, about one year before Romania. After liberation, the survivors of the camps stayed in place for several weeks to recuperate. Then they walked in convoys towards Romania, home. Often they were right behind the front lines, where street fighting, bombing, lack of food, and the taking of prisoners still threatened their lives. This trek lasted about one year.

Both of Felicia's parents survived but with chronic depression. Her grandparents and many aunts, uncles, and cousins did not survive the camp.

In May 1945, what remained of Felicia's family finally arrived in Vatra Dornei, their home. Romania was then ruled by a Communist government and many of the same people who had deported the Jewish population in 1941 were in power. Life under such a government was very restricted and dangerous.

In 1959, Felicia's family received exit documents and, like many other Jewish families, travelled to Israel. Still sick from their experiences in the camp, Felicia's parents could not handle the hot climate. An aunt in Montreal, Canada, suggested they come to live with her. Felicia lived in Montreal for her first ten years in Canada. She continued her education and ultimately received a master's degree and then, in 1985, she completed her doctorate. Felicia is married to William Thomas Cox and has a daughter, Ramona Joy Carmelly, who is an opera singer.

LAST STOP BEFORE AUSCHWITZ

· Slovakia, 1944 ·

BOB KORNHAUSER'S STORY

Left: *Bob Kornhauser's false identity card, with the name of Edmund Kolinovsky.*
Right: *Susan Jakobovic as a young girl.*

THE TRAIN WAS DEPARTING for the Auschwitz concentration camp. And Bob Kornhauser was one of hundreds of Jewish prisoners already on board. As soon as every car was full, the train would leave and the fate of every person inside would be sealed. Bob had known this even before he was pushed on board, and he already had a plan to escape. "*I won't go to Poland,*" Bob whispered into the dark and cold of the boxcar. "*I will get my freedom.*"

Bob had begun plotting his escape as soon as he and the other prisoners had arrived in Sered, the transport station from which the train was leaving for Auschwitz. Sered had been turned into a small prison camp, its perimeter controlled and policed by Slovak and German soldiers. But inside the camp, Jewish prisoners had been assigned to keep order. They distributed food and passed on the commands of the soldiers. Bob couldn't believe it when one of the first Jewish guards he bumped into was someone he knew well.

"I wish we were meeting somewhere else," Bob said when he greeted Gidali. He knew Gidali from home, and he wondered immediately if his friend might be able to help him. "I need tools," Bob whispered, glancing quickly around to see if anyone else was listening. The coast was clear. "If I have tools with me on board, I'll use them to escape."

Gidali paused and eyed the skinny young man who stood shivering in front of him. "Don't worry," he replied in hushed tones. "When we were loading straw into the train, we hid tools in every boxcar. We've taken care of it. Use the tools if you can."

There had been no time to reply. Bob and the other Jewish prisoners had been pushed forward and onto the train. More and more prisoners had been shoved inside, until there was no room to move. Finally, the doors had slid shut with a loud clang, plunging each car into darkness. Then had followed the sound of a heavy latch locking the doors in place.

Moments later, the train pulled out of the station.

Bob's mind was already at work. First, he would have to find the tools buried in the straw underneath his feet. Most of all, he needed a saw. Then, he would push his way past the other prisoners over to the wall of the boxcar next to the sliding door. He would use the saw to cut a small, square opening in the wooden wall of the car, pop it out, and reach outside. Finally, he would unhook the latch locking the door in place, and as soon as the train slowed, he would slide the door open and leap from the car, making his escape. All of this would have to happen in the time it took for the train to arrive at the next station. There was a lot to do, and no time to delay.

How many times have I gotten away from the Nazis? Bob wondered as he sank to the floor of the car and began scrounging around for the tools. Five times? Eight? Ten? He had already lost count. This last arrest was the most frustrating. It had happened on December 23, just before Christmas. Bob had been living on the streets of Bratislava then, getting by on his instincts and cunning. He had thought no one would find out about him, had believed that he might actually live out the rest of the war undetected. But as soon as he saw the Gestapo on the doorstep of the house in which he'd been hiding, his heart sank.

Bob, along with about ten others, was taken to a transit house to await deportation. Inside the house, he studied the other prisoners already assembled there—several families, young men like himself, a mother with a small child. Everyone looked lost and afraid. A young girl sat next to Bob. She had a pretty face and long, dark braids.

"What's your name?" Bob asked.

The girl looked up, startled, and then glanced at her parents and brother before replying, "Susan." She spoke in such a low voice that Bob had to lean forward to hear her. "The Gestapo beat me," Susan continued. "My mother sewed money into my coat—just in case we got separated. I was going to use it to get to safety. But the Nazis found it." She reached up to rub her shoulder and arms. Bob felt sorry for her.

"Don't worry," he said. "It will be okay." There was something about this young girl. She had strength in her eyes, and determination—two qualities that Bob knew were necessary for survival.

When the prisoners arrived in Sered, the men and women were separated. Bob lost sight of Susan in the crowded frenzy. He thought of her now and wondered which boxcar she was in.

Ah, finally, the tools! Bob thought as he wrapped his hands around a burlap bag. He tugged and the bag pulled free.

"What are you doing?" a young man next to Bob whispered in the shadows. Bob could not see his face, only his icy breath, which hung like a cloud in the frozen darkness.

"I'm breaking out," replied Bob. Quickly he explained his plan.

"Count me in," the young man said. "My name is Lustig."

"Kornhauser," Bob replied.

"I want to help as well," another voice called out in the dark. "I'm Bardos."

Within seconds, a group of prisoners had pushed forward to be included in the escape. "With more of us, there will be a better chance of success," Lustig said.

Bardos nodded. "One person can't do this alone."

Bob paused to consider this. He liked to work on his own. It was better not to rely on too many people for help. But maybe these young men were right. Sawing through the wall of the train might not be as easy as he thought. Having backup would come in handy. He nodded. "Let's go. We've wasted enough time."

Bob, Lustig, Bardos, and several other young men began to push their way through the tightly packed crowd, elbowing and shoving so that they could get to the side of the boxcar.

"Where do you think you are going?" an old man wheezed. "Sit down. Nothing is going to happen to you if you stay put."

Bob ignored the man and continued to push towards the door. He knew the passengers on this train were headed for certain death. How could this old man not know that? By now, everyone knew about the concentration camps in Poland. Death camps—that's what they were called. Bob's parents and siblings, Annie, Rose, Ilona, and Shlomo, had already been arrested and taken away. He didn't know where they were, or if they were still alive. Every nerve in Bob's body told him that he had to get out of the train before it crossed the Polish border. His instincts were strong; his determination to survive was even stronger.

Bob and the others finally reached the side of the train car. Bob dug into the burlap bag and pulled out a small saw. He held it up … and his heart sank. It would take forever to cut through the thick wooden wall of the train using this flimsy tool. Still, what choice did he have? With a deep breath, Bob turned to the wooden slats and began to saw.

He had barely begun his work when the whistle blew and the train began to slow.

"You have to stop," Lustig whispered urgently from behind. "We're arriving at the next station. We'll have to wait until the train pulls out again."

Bob paused and nodded in frustration. This was taking longer than he had thought. *How many more stops will there be before the Polish border?* he wondered. Once they reached Poland, there would be no point in trying to escape. Even if he did manage to get off the train, Bob knew that most Poles would be all too willing to turn a Jew over to the authorities. There would be no safe places to hide in Poland. His only chance would be to get off the train while it was still travelling through Slovakia. Bob knew this countryside. He knew the people. Here, he would have the best chance of getting away. But how much time did he and the others have?

The train slowed and came to a screeching stop. For a moment, everything was quiet and peaceful. And then loud shouts and gunshots cut through the stillness.

It was amazing how quickly word spread through the cars of prisoners. The Nazis were shouting from one end of the train. Within minutes, everyone knew what was happening.

"Did you hear?" a man asked. "Someone has escaped from a boxcar up ahead."

Bob sat back in amazement. Two young girls from another car had beaten him to it and managed to escape. *Good for them*, he thought, and he wondered if Susan was among the escapees. But while the news might have been good for the girls who got away, it meant more trouble for those left behind. Seconds later, the door to the boxcar slid open. Nazi guards stood outside with their guns drawn.

"We'll kill you all!" they shouted as they waved their rifles and threatened those who stood in the open doorways. "We'll shoot you dead if anyone else tries to escape."

Just in case that message wasn't loud and clear enough, the guards decided that they had better watch their prisoners more carefully. Attached to every boxcar, at the back, there was a small enclosure, a booth built for manual braking. The

Nazis placed one guard inside each enclosed area to guard the boxcar in front of him. The plan was for these guards to jump down whenever the train came to a stop and focus their guns on the doors. No prisoners were going to get away after that.

What now? Bob thought frantically as the train began to move again. The prospect of escape was growing dimmer with each passing minute.

"Got any ideas?" asked Bardos.

"We could saw through the floor," said Bob. "The Nazis are guarding the doors, but not the floor of the train."

Bardos shook his head. "The train will run you over. You'll be killed on the tracks. It's an impossible plan."

Bob and his friends racked their brains to come up with an escape plan. They talked about and rejected idea after idea, until there were no ideas left. Through the small window above Bob's head, he could see that they were approaching the Polish border. The next station would be Zilina, the last stop before Poland and Auschwitz.

"It's over," Bob sighed. He stared out the window, knowing that there was no point any more in trying to escape. *I've done everything I can do*, he thought. *I've run out of ideas, run out of plans, run out of running!* It was amazing how the spirit to fight could be so strong one minute and then gone the next. Bob's fire had simply gone out, replaced with a calm resignation.

He reached into his pocket and pulled out a piece of bread, smiling in spite of himself. There had been no food for the prisoners on this ride to Auschwitz. But somehow, Bob always managed to find bread in his pockets. And if he managed to get a new piece of bread, he would throw out the old one. Bob chewed slowly and settled back into the straw. *What will be, will be,* he thought. He was not afraid. He felt at peace. He had fought hard all his life, and now he was tired. He closed his eyes. *When I wake up, I'll be in Auschwitz.* Those were Bob's last thoughts before he drifted off to sleep.

BOB AWOKE WITH A START. How long had he been sleeping? He glanced out the window. It was still dark, but something caught his eye. The train was passing through a small station and the name of the town lit up as it appeared in the window of the boxcar. This was a Czech town. With a gasp, Bob realized that the train was not in Poland at all. Somehow, it had been diverted, and was now travelling through Czechoslovakia. He didn't know that the Nazis were already in retreat from Auschwitz and other concentration camps. The Nazis had all but lost the war, and the concentration camps were being liquidated as the Nazis were moving their prisoners deep into Germany and other countries, trying not to leave behind any evidence of their atrocities. All Bob knew was that one moment the train had been taking him to his death, and the next moment he had been granted a reprieve. This was a sign, an omen, and Bob sprang to his feet with a renewed determination to get out of the train.

"Lustig," he said, shaking him awake. "Look! The train isn't in Poland. If we get out now, the Czechs will help us for sure. We've got a chance again. Are you coming with me?"

Lustig rubbed his eyes and nodded enthusiastically, followed by Bardos, who was listening in. Soon, there were ten young men, all resolved to escape from the train. But how? There was still the problem of the Nazi guards who were patrolling carefully at every train stop. Besides, the men no longer had their tools. When the girls had escaped from the train, Bob and the others had quickly thrown their tools out the window, afraid that the Nazis would search the boxcars and discover them. Without tools, how could they possibly get away?

In the fight to survive, decisions had to be made from minute to minute, not even hour to hour, let alone day to day. Bob knew this from years of having made life-and-death decisions. You couldn't be afraid, only grateful in the moment to still be safe, and fighting for life. This was one of those moments, and Bob knew he had to think quickly. He glanced out the small window, stretching to catch sight of the moon, anxious to determine how long he had before the sun would rise and all thoughts of escape would have to be abandoned once more. Bob stared at the window, long and hard, and suddenly he knew what he was going to do.

The window was small, and it had no glass, but it did have horizontal bars. Bob examined the bars carefully. *If I can squeeze my head through those bars*, he thought, *then the rest of my body will follow.* Quickly, Bob shared his plan with his friends. He would push his head and shoulders through the bars in the window while the other men held his legs. Then, he would reach over to the sliding door and unhook the latch to open the door so they could make their getaway. This all had to happen quickly, before daylight, and before the guards jumped out of their small enclosures to watch the doors.

Bob peeled off his heavy coat, shivering in the icy coldness that instantly penetrated his body. He stripped down to his undershirt and reached up to the bars of the window. It would be a tight squeeze, he thought, and then he quickly pushed all doubt from his mind. Bob pressed his head sideways against the bars. He forced the top of his head through and then carefully twisted his ears against the cold, rigid steel, wincing as the rough metal pressed and scraped against his cheek. Inch by inch, like a serpent, he wriggled and squirmed, slowly manoeuvring his body through the narrow gap. And with a final push, the top half of Bob's body was outside the train. The wintry wind nearly took his breath away. The train was not moving quickly, but without the protection of his coat, Bob's body began to shake in the bitter cold.

"Hold on to my legs," he called out behind him as he doubled over and hung his body forward, trying to reach for the hook on the door. Bob grasped at the latch and pulled while icy tears blinded his eyes. His fingers were already numb. One tug, then another, and with a final cry, Bob pulled the hook up and off the door.

"I've done it! It's unlocked!" he shouted triumphantly to his friends in the train. "Pull me back."

The other men tugged and pulled, and finally they managed to squeeze Bob through the bars and back inside the car. When he stepped over to the train door and slid it open, full moonlight streamed into the boxcar, nearly blinding him. It was the most beautiful sight he could ever have imagined. Out there was freedom and a chance at life. Hastily, Bob pulled his coat back on. The cold air from outside circulated throughout the train car.

"Sit down!" a prisoner shouted. "You're going to get us all killed."

"What do you think you are doing?" another one demanded. "Don't make any trouble and we'll be fine."

"Listen," said Bob, turning to face the prisoners. "We're getting out of here. And anyone is welcome to join us."

With that, Bob turned back to the door. The train was swaying and lurching from side to side, and he held on to the wall beside the open door, trying to steady himself. There were two steps down from the boxcar, and Bob carefully moved onto the first step. He was just about to jump when a train whizzed by in the opposite direction. Bob clutched at the door and held on with all his might. Had he jumped at that moment, the oncoming train would have crushed him. But, once again, he was safe.

Regaining his balance, Bob looked out at the countryside and at the moon that glowed with the promise of freedom. *I know how to do this*, he said to himself, thinking back to his childhood. As a youngster, Bob had often jumped off the streetcars in Bratislava to avoid paying the fare. Then, it had all been a reckless game. Now, it was a matter of life and death.

Bob glanced over his shoulder at his friends, still inside the boxcar. "We'll meet up beside the track," he shouted, and then turned and hurled himself forward off the train.

Bob rolled once, then once more. He had used his arms to shield his head, and as he lay in the gravel by the side of the train tracks, he knew he was not hurt. He sat up and looked behind him. The train did not slow down. No one had seen him escape. The red lights of the caboose were disappearing into the distance. Bob knew that he was safe once more.

POSTSCRIPT

In total, Bob managed to either escape from or elude arrest by the Nazis eleven times. After this escape from the train,

Bob eventually made his way back to Bratislava, along with his new friends Lustig and Bardos. He obtained false papers that identified him as Edmund Kolinovsky. Using these documents, Bob travelled to Nitra and was finally liberated there by the Soviet army. He then returned to Bratislava and worked with an organization that provided aid to Jewish survivors returning from the concentration camps. He discovered that, of his immediate family, only his sister, Annie, and his mother had survived the camps.

One day, Bob met a young woman on the streets of Bratislava. Her name was Susan Jakobovic—it was the same young woman he had met before being put on the train to Auschwitz. Susan had survived the Ravensbruck concentration camp. Susan and Bob married in 1948. They lived in Israel until 1958, when they immigrated to Canada. They have two sons and three grandchildren.

A FIRST DAY

• Auschwitz-Birkenau, 1944 •
JUDY WEISSENBERG COHEN'S STORY

*Judy, four years old, on the right with Klara, ten, in the middle
and Eva, six, on the left.*

"ELIZABETH, I CAN'T HOLD IT. I have to go." Judy tried not to complain but the constant jostling of the train rattled her insides. At least there was no need to squish her knees together, not with seventy or more people pressed up against each other. She could hardly breathe, let alone move.

Where were they going? Everyone asked the same question. "North," was Elizabeth's best guess. They had left Debrecen, Hungary, on June 29, 1944. How many days had passed? Three? No, four. That would mean that today was July 3, maybe. It was hard to think. They had been standing for four days. There was no room to sit, not even for a moment. The old people perched on suitcases with children on their laps. The rest stood. Their knees often buckled, but the sheer press of people kept them upright.

There were six people in Judy's immediate family on the train: her mother, Anyu, and her father, Apu, plus Judy and her three sisters. Elizabeth, more like a mother than a big sister, was twenty-seven years old; Klara was twenty-two; Eva was eighteen. Judy was the youngest, the baby. She was fifteen years old. Their three brothers were not with them. They had already been taken away as slave labourers for the Hungarian army. Apu, her pious, gentle father, and Anyu were worn down with worry.

After her brothers were taken away, the Gestapo had ordered Apu to report to headquarters for interrogation. They wanted gold. What gold? The family—all Jewish families, rich or poor—had already been stripped of their valuables. But the Nazis believed all Jews had gold, squirrelled away someplace. Where? Under floorboards, perhaps? In the attic, maybe? If they'd had gold, would Apu not have used it to bribe their way out of Hungary the moment the Germans had stomped into their country? No, no, they had no gold, but the Gestapo cruelly beat the soles of Apu's feet anyway.

The train took a curve and everyone in the car swayed back and forth. Peeking between bobbing chins and heads, faces with tear-stained cheeks and quivering lips, Judy could almost hear Apu's prayer: "*Shema Yisrael, Adonai Eloheinu, Adonai Echad.*"[2] Apu spoke Hebrew to God. Over and over he pleaded with Him to save his family. Apu prayed continually now, although his prayers did not seem to bring him peace or hope.

"Elizabeth, I must go. I must," Judy whispered.

"Come, I'll help you get to the bucket." Elizabeth wriggled her arm around Judy's waist and pulled her in close.

Almost all of her aunts and uncles and her thirty cousins, including tiny children and even babies, were in the same cattle car. Judy's beautiful sister-in-law, Magda, and her blond, blue-eyed baby boy, Peter, were there too. There were lots of small children in the cattle car, but it was quiet now. Even the babies seemed to have fallen into a stupor.

Slowly, Elizabeth and Judy inched towards the door of the cattle car. The first time she had tried to use the bucket had been completely humiliating. To expose herself like that—it was indecent! If only they would get to wherever they were going. There couldn't be any place more horrible than this!

Judy hovered over the bucket while Elizabeth used her body as a shield—not that anyone was looking. The stench of

---

[2]"Hear, O Israel, the Lord our God, the Lord is one."

the bucket was overpowering. It had been emptied only once. That would have been two days ago, maybe. It was so hard to keep track, but she remembered the sound of the cattle cars being unlocked—*crack, crack, crack*—and then the doors rattling on the rails, the noise echoing like rolling thunder.

"Are you done?" Elizabeth spoke over her shoulder.

"Yes." Judy braced one hand against the wall of the car and pulled up her underpants. There was a sound—a long, lone screech—as the train wheels braked. The train was stopping.

"Come, hold on to me." Elizabeth reached out and grabbed her little sister. There was a moment of silence and then, as the doors of the cattle car rumbled opened, there was chaos.

"*Los, los, heraus, schneller!*"[3] The blast of cool, early-morning air flooded the cattle car. "*Los, los, heraus, schneller!*" Men wearing what looked like funny striped pyjamas jumped up into the car and began pulling and shoving. "*Los, los!*" Young and old tumbled out of the car onto a raised, wooden platform. "*Los, los!*" The shouts of the men mingled with the cries of babies and the screams of frightened children.

"Anyu!" Judy cried. Everyone was calling out for each other. "Apu!" Judy screamed so loud that the effort scratched her throat.

---

[3] "Go, go, out, faster!"

"*Los, los, heraus, schneller!* Leave all your belongings in the car!" There were dogs on the platform—large, vicious German shepherds straining against thick black straps held by German soldiers. The dogs barked, growled, leapt up, and every so often bit into exposed flesh.

What was happening? "Elizabeth? Eva?" Judy cried out. Where was she? Where had her sisters gone?

"I'm here. Hold on to me." Elizabeth grabbed Judy's hand. "Klara, Eva," Elizabeth cried. "Hold on to Anyu and Apu." The panic and the screams drowned out Elizabeth's voice.

"Get in line!" the men in striped pyjamas shouted in Yiddish and German. They pushed and shoved, all the while muttering to the young mothers under their breath, "*Give the children to the grandmothers. Give the babies to the grandmothers.*"

"What are they saying?" Judy half cried, half whispered as they jostled for space on the platform.

"I don't know," said Elizabeth as she stood on her toes and strained to find their parents. "Klara, Klara, come." She beckoned frantically, her hand waving like a flag.

Judy twisted around. Where was Apu? Where had he gone? "Apu!" she screamed, again and again. "Apu!"

"Quiet," the man in the striped pyjamas growled.

Wait, something was wrong. All the men had been taken away! Apu, her father, was gone. They had been separated out and pulled away, before anyone knew what was happening. "Where did he go? Apu, APU!" Judy cried.

Elizabeth wasn't listening. "Klara, Klara, come." With one hand Elizabeth hung on to Judy and with the other she pulled their mother and Klara and Eva towards her. Anyu reached for her daughter-in-law, who held her baby tightly.

"Your father, where is your father?" cried Anyu. First her sons were taken, and now her husband was gone and her daughters were in danger. "*Einziger Gott in Himmel*," Anya whispered in German. "*Our only God in Heaven, protect us.*"

"Quiet!" the man in the striped pyjamas yelled over and over.

At last, all the women and children from the train stood in a line, four, five, or six abreast. Anyu stood behind her daughters and beside her daughter-in-law and grandson Peter, her sister-in-law, and cousins.

"Hush, Anyu, we'll see him soon," Elizabeth hissed over her shoulder.

"Where are we?" Judy whispered.

"I don't know."

Behind them was the open cattle car; in front of them were high-ranking German officers. There was no sun, yet the buttons and boots of the SS officers sparkled. They were dressed impeccably. Especially compared to the poor people tumbling out of the cattle cars, the officers looked well fed and healthy. They strutted about as though they didn't have a care in the world.

Judy looked down at her own worn shoes. She had seen German officers before but from a distance, not like this, not up close. They were frightening, as frightening as the dogs that tugged against the leather straps.

The line moved forward. The girls were shoved ahead until Elizabeth, Judy, Eva, and Klara stood directly in front of a German SS officer. He wore clean, snow-white gloves. Judy could see his thumbs gesturing to the right or the left as he looked each person up and down. What could it mean?

While he inspected the four girls, Judy stared only at his thumbs. *Right, right, right, right* went the thumb. The four girls were shoved aside by the men in the striped pyjamas. Judy looked back. Anyu and Magda, along with other women holding small children, now stood in front of the German officer. Baby Peter whimpered as he laid his head on his mother's shoulder. *Left, left, left, left* went the thumb. "Anyu!" Eva cried. There was no time to speak or even look back as their mother, sister-in-law, baby nephew, and little cousins were pushed along the platform. And as suddenly as their father had disappeared, so too went their mother. Gone. What had just happened? Where was Anyu going?

"She's with Magda. It will be all right," Elizabeth whispered as they were hustled farther and farther to the right, off the platform towards a large, solid, grey cement building.

"Anyu, Anyu," Judy whispered as she twisted around, eyes wide. What could Magda do to help their mother? What could any of them do? Eva and Klara held on to each other while Elizabeth gripped Judy's hand.

"*Schnell, schnell!*" yelled more men in striped pyjamas. There were woman yelling too, all dressed in striped shifts, all thin and angry—pushing, yelling, more pushing, more yelling. "Move, move!"

"Remove your clothes. *Schnell!*"

What did he say? The girls, everyone, stood in shock. Remove their clothes … out here? In front of men?

"*SCHNELL!*"

A woman down the line refused. Her refusal was met with a strap to the back. Again she refused. Then came a blow to her head. She crumpled to the ground.

"Come, do as they say." Amid the sobs of the women and the barking of the dogs, Elizabeth's voice was soft and comforting. As if to prove that it could be done, Elizabeth tossed her coat onto a pile of clothes, then pulled her dress and her slip over her head. *There*, she seemed to say, *I can do it, so can you.*

Judy sucked in her breath. Elizabeth was skinny. She had been in Palestine for many years but she had become ill with malaria, so ill that she'd had to return home. She was a *woman of the world* to her sisters, wise beyond her years, smart, resourceful—yet now she looked so small in her undergarments. What if she had stayed in Palestine? What if she had never come home? *Elizabeth, I wish you were still safe in Palestine, but I am glad you are here taking care of us.* The two thoughts collided in Judy's mind as she tried not to cry, tried not scream.

"Everything. Remove everything. Just keep your shoes on," snarled a short, squat, fair-haired woman dressed in a German uniform. Undaunted, Elizabeth removed the rest of her clothing and again threw it onto the heap.

"Come." Elizabeth unbuttoned the top buttons on Judy's dress before turning to help Eva, and then Klara. "Just do as they say," she hissed into her sisters' ears.

None of them had ever been naked in front of each other, let alone strangers, and to stand there, like that, in front of that German woman and the strange men ... *any* men! It was more shameful than the bucket on the train, more shameful than anything. Judy crossed her arms over her chest. She'd have cried if she'd had the tears, if her teeth would have stopped chattering.

"Move, *schnell!*" More yelling, more pushing, more dogs barking.

A door to the large, ugly cement building opened and they went in, tripping and stumbling over each other.

The room was cold; the cement floor under their feet was damp.

Men and women in striped pyjamas stood behind long, rough benches. They held scissors and razors. Why? What would they need them for?

"MOVE!" The soldiers used rifle butts to propel the naked women forward while the men and women in striped clothes used their hands to push and shove.

Judy looked up. Bare light bulbs hung from the rafters. It was a nightmare. She would wake up soon and be home in her own bed. This couldn't be real. What had they done to deserve this? The room seemed to spin.

"MOVE!"

There was something soft under her feet, almost warm compared to the cement floor. Judy looked down. Hair, human hair. They were cutting off hair! She could feel a scream rise up in her throat but it didn't come out. Nothing came out.

The razor nicked her scalp. The hair fell off, her beautiful chestnut hair! They shaved off all hair. Nicks and cuts appeared all over her body. Then there was a splash. For a moment the world went white, white with searing pain. Ammonia cleaner seeped into the cuts. Her body was burning. She doubled over with pain.

"*Schnell. SCHNELL!* MOVE!" yelled a disembodied voice.

Another door opened. Where were her sisters? Elizabeth? Klara? Where were they? Eva?

The shaving room led into another. Dozens and dozens of

women were packed into an empty chamber. Where were they now? The door slammed shut behind them. Shower heads hung from long pipes that ran the length of the ceiling. And then, before there was time to take it in, freezing-cold water sprayed from above. Judy moaned as she lifted her arms and tried, tried to rub off the stinging ammonia. She opened her mouth to catch water but her chattering teeth prevented even a few drops from dribbling down her throat. And then the water stopped and a far door opened.

"*Schnell, SCHNELL!*"

With watery eyes and wet skin, Judy peered out. There were no trees, no grass, nothing that looked like earth. They were in another place, somewhere not of the world. Judy stumbled and turned. Around her stood frail, bald, naked women. All were bewildered, dazed, and unable to recognize each other.

"Elizabeth, where are you? Eva? Klara?" Judy whispered. Gone. Vanished. Like Apu and Anyu. She was alone. Alone. *Please, please, don't leave me alone in this place.* "ELIZABETH?"

"Here, here I am. Hush, hush." Elizabeth folded her arms around her little sister. "We're all here."

Judy stumbled back, astonished. "Elizabeth?"

"Yes, it's me."

She hadn't recognized her. Only her eyes and her voice were familiar. Judy reached up and touched her sister's face. "Elizabeth?"

"Yes, yes, hush. It's me."

Then Eva stumbled towards them. "Eva? And Klara?" cried Judy. "Is that you?"

All four sisters looked at each other, speechless. Eva, as beautiful as a girl in a storybook, and Klara, oh lovely, lovely Klara, with doe-soft eyes as dark as chocolates. Elizabeth, not beautiful like Eva, and not enchanting like Klara, but striking all the same, she was the warrior queen. She was fierce and strong, not in body maybe, but in spirit. But now …?

Again the guards yelled. What were they to do? There were no towels, just a huge heap of cast-off clothes. A woman in the striped shift tossed bits of clothing to each person as the other men and women in striped pyjamas forced them forward. A lady's nightgown, thin and blue with tiny flowers, fell into Judy's hands. She scrambled into it and instantly it became damp. The hem of the nightgown fell to the ground.

"Come here." Elizabeth gathered her three sisters around her. "Stand still, Judy." She bent down, and gripping the material that fell beneath Judy's knee, she ripped. Holding the remnant up she ripped it again and again until she held four narrow strips of cloth. "Wind it around your head, like this." Elizabeth took one strip and wrapped it around her head twice, tied it off, and tucked in the ends. Quickly each girl did likewise, and for a moment, they took back what little they could of their dignity.

With their shoes gathered in their arms, all the women were pushed into a wooden building. There seemed to be fifty, maybe sixty of them. There were no chairs, no bunks, no blankets, nothing.

"Will we get food?" Eva whispered.

"They seem to want to keep us alive, and that means that they have to feed us at some point. Here, sit." Elizabeth, big sister, again took charge. With their backs against the wall, the four girls sat and waited.

There was food, if the slimy, grey, watery stuff that smelled too foul to eat could be called that. One bowl was handed out to every five women. There were no utensils for scooping up the liquid. Each was expected to take a gulp and pass the bowl around in a circle. All three girls turned away from the revolting, runny stew.

"No, I can't." It was Klara who said no first, and then Judy and Eva.

"Eat." Elizabeth's voice rose up over the whimpers and cries. "If you are to stay alive you must eat." Still the three refused.

Elizabeth got up and walked towards the door.

"Where are you going?" Judy leaped forward. She could bear anything, anything, as long as she had her sisters.

"I'll be back." Elizabeth waded through the women as they all tried to choke back the contents of the bowl.

"Where are we?" Judy could hear Elizabeth ask a stone-faced woman. The woman shook her head. "What is this place called?" Elizabeth asked again and again. No one knew. Elizabeth stomped her foot. "Country? What country is this?"

A woman by the door grinned and stamped her foot too. "Poland. This," she waved, "is Auschwitz-Birkenau." The woman spoke with a thick accent but not one Judy could easily place.

"It is a camp, a labour camp, is it not?"

Judy crept closer to hear better. A sick feeling curled in her stomach. There had been rumours back in Hungary about camps where people were killed, murdered. But they were only rumours spread by unreliable people who wanted to cause panic. *It's not possible, it's not possible. Not even the Nazis …*

"There is work and much more," replied the woman, with a sniff. "You came in back way. You lucky. Before, they tattoo numbers on arms. Now, not so much. Too busy."

"What is that smell?" asked Elizabeth. It was a putrid, awful stench that was hard to identify. But as she took in another breath, Judy's heart began to pound.

The woman grimaced, then pointed to orange flames leaping out of far chimneys. "Over there—the ovens," was all she said before turning away.

"Elizabeth?" whispered Judy. "Don't leave us."

Elizabeth crept out of the building. Where did she go?

The girls dozed off. It was not a sleep exactly, more an uncomfortable nap filled with dark images and fear. It was an hour, maybe more, maybe less, before Elizabeth returned carrying a piece of soft wood and what might have been, in more civil times, a butter knife. Startled, Judy woke up and looked up at her sister with such relief that she silently prayed, *Thank you, God.*

Elizabeth sat with the wood between her knees and carefully, over the next few hours, carved out four wooden spoons while her three sisters slept. When the girls awoke, Elizabeth passed out wooden spoons to each girl, then took up the half-empty bowl of filthy bile and said, "Now, you will eat."

Later, lying on the floor back to back in rows, they all tried to sleep. Only Judy sat awake, wide-eyed, disoriented, and filled with terror.

"Anyu, Apu," Judy whispered. "Mother, Father, where are you?" Round, salty tears slid down her face. It would be the last time, until liberation, that Judy would cry.

POSTSCRIPT

Of Judy Weissenberg Cohen's family of nine, only she and two of her siblings—brother Leslie and sister Eva—survived. Judy is now married to Sidney Jessel Cohen and they have two children, Michelle and Jonathan. Judy is a recipient of the Ontario Volunteers Award and creator and editor of the award-winning website "Women and the Holocaust." Through her public speaking, she is an activist on issues related to the Holocaust and other past and current genocides.

ONE POTATO, TWO POTATO

• Camp somewhere in Poland, 1944 •

FANNY FRYDMAN PILLERSDORF'S STORY

"FANNY, THERE IS WORK. There are boys and girls shovelling snow. You must go."

My papa, Yosek Itzak, the baker, stood at the door of our apartment and made this announcement loudly. He hardly ever raised his voice. Papa was a kind and gentle man, but nothing and no one was the same any more—not even Mama or my two little sisters, Pearl and Tsuti. Everyone was nervous. But mostly we were all very, *very* hungry.

The Germans had marched into my city of Dabrowa, Poland, with their big boots and guns on September 1, 1939. At first I'd thought them handsome in their perfectly pressed uniforms with sparkling buttons. Then everything had changed. Overnight, Jews became the enemy—not only to the Germans, but to the Polish people also. How could that be? I was Jewish, but I was Polish too! What did it matter what religion we practised? We were all Polish. We all loved our country.

And it wasn't just the Jews that the Germans hated. My principal, Mr. Lewicki, wasn't Jewish, but the Germans took him away to a concentration camp anyway because they said that he was a Jewish sympathizer and a Polish patriot. I was only fourteen but I wondered why the Germans and so *many* Poles hated us? I'm a grandma now, and I still wonder why. It was all so long ago, but sometimes it seems that it happened yesterday.

Just as Papa suggested, I volunteered to shovel snow. I was happy to do it. I wanted to do something useful. I wanted to help my country. I can remember saying goodbye to my parents that day and joining the other boys and girls on the street shovelling mountains of snow away from the sidewalks and road.

A truck came down the road and all of us children were ordered into the back. "*Schnell! Schnell!*" The Germans were always yelling. We did what we were told and climbed into the truck. At first we were not afraid. We thought that we were just going to another place to shovel snow. But the truck kept going, on and on. What was happening? How would we get home before dark? My heart started to race. I became more and more anxious. What about my parents? They would be so worried.

Finally we arrived at a little labour camp.

It was a collection of wooden buildings surrounded by wire. There was a POW camp attached, filled with prisoners of war, men fighting Hitler. We could see them through the wire fences. They didn't look very healthy, but I thought them brave and wonderful anyway. Sometimes they would throw apples and bread over to us. Maybe we didn't look very healthy to *them*. They told us to hang on, not to give up hope. They said the war would soon be over and we would be free.

I was sent to work in the kitchen to peel potatoes, one barrel a day. At the end of the day I would hide a potato or two in my panties and smuggle them into the barracks. I tried my best to share everything—all the girls who worked in the kitchen did the same. It was very dangerous. If we were caught stealing we could be shot on the spot.

The commandant was a short little man, old to me, maybe fifty. He carried a stick under his arm and he would use it to poke us. Many times we were made to stand naked in front of the commandant and other officers. I was humiliated. We would stand in a line and the officers would walk past us, looking us up and down. If there were any marks on our bodies, even a cut that was not healing quickly, we would be sent to a death camp.

Line up and be counted. Line up and be counted. They counted us and recounted us, once, twice, sometimes three times a day. It didn't matter how cold it was, and they often left us standing in freezing weather with hardly any clothes on. That's when it happened.

I had peeled my quota of potatoes that day and, like many times before, I'd tucked a potato into my underpants. I was on my way back to the barracks when we were told to line up to be counted. We stood with our shoulders back, trying to look strong and healthy even though we were exhausted and starving. And then, as the commandant walked in front of me, the potato fell out and rolled on the ground.

There was silence. He stopped and looked me up and down, and then his face grew fierce and contorted as he raised his hand in the air. His stick came down on one side of my face and then the other. My cheeks were on fire. He was grunting as he whipped me again and again. But that wasn't good enough. I don't know if the stick broke or he threw it down but he started to slap me. Slapping wasn't good enough either. He curled up his fist and punched me in the eyes, in the mouth, all over my head, over and over. Blood was dripping down my face onto my dress. It was in my eyes, but I couldn't wipe it away. With each punch he yelled dirty things at me, awful things, words I cannot repeat. Over and over and over, screaming, hitting. I couldn't defend myself. I couldn't put my hands up. He kept going and going until he was exhausted. And then he said, in a low, hissing voice, "If you ever steal another potato you will be killed."

The next day my face was swollen and my eyes could hardly open, but I returned to the kitchen to peel potatoes. And that same day—I stole another potato.

POSTSCRIPT

Fanny survived seven camps before running away from a death march. She hid with three other girls until liberation, three weeks later.

With the exception of two aunts, Fanny Frydman Pillersdorf's family, including her two little sisters, were murdered by the German Nazis. Today, Fanny lives in Toronto with her husband, Leib Pillersdorf, also a Holocaust survivor. They have three children: one is a doctor, another a dentist, and the third a physiotherapist. They also have three grandchildren.

JUDGMENT DAY

· Ravensbruck, 1942 ·

ARTHUR KACER'S STORY

Arthur Kacer as a young man after the war.

SHE WAS STARING AGAIN. Staring at me. The hatred in her eyes sent a shiver down my spine. I stiffened, turned away, and tried to focus on the work in front of me, but I could still feel her eyes burning into my back. She did not know me, and yet she loathed me so completely. I called her "the Hawk," a fitting name. She was the stalker and I was her prey.

That day was no different from any other day. A prisoner in the Ravensbruck concentration camp, I had been working in the nearby airplane factory for several months. My job was to review the blueprints for a new airplane that was being built for Hitler's armies. I would help with the design of the plane while others constructed the parts, according to the plans. It was a complicated job, especially for a young man like me, a prisoner, and my life depended on my ability to do the work and do it well.

I suppose I was luckier than many. I was young and strong—fit from years of outdoor sports like soccer. But more importantly, I had a trade, one that was valuable to the Nazis. I knew how to design plans for automobiles and airplanes. I had worked with my father as an apprentice and learned everything about drafting. And it was that skill that saved my life the day I first arrived in Ravensbruck.

It was a crisp, sunny afternoon in late October 1942. Our freight train had rumbled to a stop on the rails inside the concentration camp, and the doors of each cattle car had been violently thrown open by Nazi SS soldiers carrying machine guns.

"*Heraus, heraus.* Out, out!" they shouted.

I hurried down the ramp under a rain of clubs and past the snapping, barking jaws of angry German shepherds. It had taken five days to reach this camp in Germany from my home in Czechoslovakia—a journey without food, water, or even fresh air. I was dazed, hungry, and frightened. After all, I had left my family and friends far behind, and I had no idea what this place was, or what I would find here. All I knew was that it could not be good.

The air was thick with the deafening and confusing sound of orders being bellowed and dogs barking. I shivered and lined up with the others for my introduction to life in the concentration camp: the selection. The SS officer paced at the end of the platform, and as each prisoner passed before him, he gestured to the right or to the left. He had a handsome face, even a pleasant smile. But he held the power of life and death in his hands.

When my turn came, I stood tall and thrust my shoulders back and said, "I have many skills, *Obersturmführer*," addressing the officer by title. I spoke in the perfect German I had learned in school.

The SS officer paused. A smirk passed over his lips and his gaze returned to settle on me. "What skills would a Jew have?" he asked.

I gulped, knowing I was taking a chance. Volunteering to speak got you noticed, and being noticed could backfire and get you killed on the spot. But somehow, I knew I had to take this gamble. "I've studied drafting, *Obersturmführer*," I continued. "I understand plans for machinery. I can read blueprints for airplanes. I can be useful."

The officer gazed at me a moment longer, and then pointed to the left. My life was spared. Those too weak or sick were herded back onto the trains. I knew they were doomed and I would not see them again. They were to be transferred to another concentration camp where they would be put to death. The rest of us were assigned to work in the factory.

I saw the Hawk on my very first day. How could I not notice her? She stood in the open window between the office and the workplace, supervising the prisoners in the factory. She barely moved her body, but her eyes followed me everywhere. They were haunting eyes, seething eyes that smouldered like burning embers. She stood, framed in that opening, as if an artist had painted her life-sized portrait and hung it there. She stood out, not only for her hatred, but because everything else about this woman was out of place in the dirt and squalor of the prison. Her brown, wavy hair was perfectly combed and stylish. Her uniform was clean, and occasionally I caught a whiff of her perfume, which reminded me of my older sister.

"Who is she?" I whispered to an inmate standing close by. We were not allowed to speak and could be beaten for breaking this rule. But we prisoners were resourceful and had learned ways to communicate and not be noticed. Like a brief Morse code, we muttered clipped messages to one another whenever and wherever we could.

"Her husband is an SS captain on the Soviet front," the man replied, as he wheezed and coughed into his ragged sleeve. He wiped his mouth and added, "Stay away from her. The hateful ones are the most dangerous of all."

I nodded and returned to my work, troubled by what the man had said. *Why did this woman hate us so?* I wondered. I had done nothing to her or to the other Nazi guards in the prison. I had not harmed my friends back home who had turned on me, or the shopkeepers who had refused to let me into their stores, or my teachers who had snarled and banned me from the classroom. I had done nothing to any of them, and yet they hated me and wanted me dead. Jews, they said, were a disease, an infection that had to be destroyed. *Judenfrei.* That was what Hitler wanted for the world. *Judenfrei*—free of Jews. Hitler and his followers had taught a nation to hate us just because of our religion. And he was so powerful and so convincing that the people believed his every word and followed his ranting. *If Hitler had said, "It's the soccer players who need to be destroyed," would everyone have believed that too?* I wondered scornfully as I tried to focus on my work.

I knew I had to stay out of the Hawk's way. My fellow prisoner's warning rang in my ears—"*the hateful ones are the most dangerous of all.*" And I had a chance to see just how dangerous several days later. It was late in the day and I was exhausted. My body ached from the hours of unrelenting work and the lack of food. My frozen fingers were cut and bleeding. My eyes burned from staring at the detailed plans for the airplane. And in a moment of complete exhaustion, I sank to the floor of the factory and buried my head in my arms. *Just for a moment,* I thought. *I'll close my eyes for a moment and then I'll get back to work.*

But the Hawk saw me, and in a second, she stood above me screeching and waving her arms. "You think you're on vacation?" she shrieked. "Nobody said you could rest!" I stumbled to my feet and hung my head, quivering with fear. "No food rations for tonight," she screamed, before turning on her heel and marching back to her station.

This was the worst punishment, worse than standing in the cold for hours, or being beaten. The food in Ravensbruck was disgusting at the best of times, and there was little of it. But food was life, and that night my belly ached even more than usual. How would I ever make it through the next day?

I tried to avoid her the next morning, tried to stop myself from being aware of her behind me, staring at my every move. There was too much to do that day. An SS general was arriving from Berlin to check the airplane parts that the other prisoners had built. Everything had to be in perfect order for his inspection. I had to stay focused, despite the watchful eyes of this woman, as well as those of the Nazi guards, and their ever-present dogs. I could not falter in my step, or pause to rest.

"*Achtung!* Attention!" The SS general had arrived and we were ordered to line up for the inspection. The Hawk glared at me one more time before assuming her place at the front of the line and marching all of the prisoners outside.

The wind in the courtyard whipped in all directions, blowing dirt and dust into my face. The cold pierced through the thin rags of my prisoner's uniform, slicing into my body like shards of glass. I bent my head and marched quickly to stand with the other prisoners.

In front of me, the general walked from one end of the field to the other, bending to look at the airplane parts and leaning his head closer to the Hawk, who guided him around the field and spoke to him about the construction. The general wore a long, grey overcoat and carried a short riding crop that he slapped mindlessly into the palm of his hand. His black boots squeaked as he passed by. I shivered, longing for a coat like his that might protect me from the frosty air.

"This is fine work, Madam Comrade," the general said, pausing in front of me as he continued his inspection. "I will need to dictate a letter back to our headquarters, telling them that the job has been completed satisfactorily."

The Hawk looked over the gathering of prisoners, her gaze coming to rest on me. "You!" she snapped. "There is a typewriter in the office. Get it!"

I turned and ran back into the office, searching everywhere for the typewriter. Ah, there it was, sitting in a corner of the room. Clutching it and some paper to my chest, I ran out to the SS general and to the Hawk. I was about to step back in line, but just then, something overcame me. It was just like the time I had spoken out during the selection on the day I arrived in Ravensbruck. As I handed the Hawk the typewriter, I blurted out, "I can type, *Obersturmführer*."

What was I thinking? Even as the words left my mouth, I wished I could pull them back, get back in line, and become invisible once more. But it was too late. I waited, ready for the beating that was bound to follow my bold and reckless behaviour.

The Hawk froze and stared back at me as the SS general nodded in my direction. Without another word, I sank to my knees and, with trembling hands, inserted the paper into the typewriter as the general began to dictate his letter. I completed the dictation perfectly and handed the letter back. Cautiously I looked up and into the face of the woman, and for the first time, I noticed that her eyes were not filled with fury. They were curious—even a bit interested. It caught me off guard. But I had no time to ponder her expression. The general was about to leave. The inspection had been a success, and I knew that my life was spared once more.

The next day, the Hawk appeared in the factory as usual. When the other SS guards were looking elsewhere, she approached me. Out of the corner of my eye, I could see her coming from across the room, and my heart began to pound with fear. Had I done something wrong? Had she noticed me speaking to another prisoner? Was she going to report me to the guards? I bent my head, praying that she would pass. But she stopped directly in front of me and began to speak.

"I have been watching you a long time," she said stiffly, bending her head and leaning in. I could smell her perfume, could feel her breath close to me. "I notice that you behave quite normally," she continued. "You understand the plans for the construction of the airplane. You can type and read. You can even speak German."

I blinked and gulped. *Where was this going?* I wondered as I gazed back at her.

"I was told that Jews were ignorant people," she blurted. "But I do not think you are."

How to respond? I almost laughed out loud, wondering who, indeed, was the more ignorant of the two of us. I looked at this woman, stared at her as she had stared at me for months. "Listen to me," I finally replied. "We Jews are as intelligent as German people, some more, some less."

The Hawk seemed genuinely surprised, as if she were hearing something completely new, something that did not fit at all with her previous thoughts and beliefs. Had she ever really looked at a Jewish person before? Had she ever spoken to a Jew? We had existed only as animals in her mind, unworthy, unimportant.

She paused a moment longer. Then, before turning to go, she reached into her pocket and pulled out a slice of bread. Peering over her shoulder to make sure no one was watching, she placed the bread in front of me, then walked away.

For a moment, I stared at this peace offering and shook my head in amazement. Had something really changed here? Would this woman look differently at me from now on? Would she think me more of a human being—perhaps even her equal? I glanced around quickly, grabbed the bread, and returned to my work.

POSTSCRIPT

Ravensbruck was the only major Nazi concentration camp for women. In addition, it had a small camp for men, which was totally isolated from the women's camp. A high wall enclosed the whole camp, with electrified barbed wire on the top. There were also a number of sub-camps surrounding Ravensbruck, from which prisoners were sent to work in factories producing arms and other equipment for the Nazis. Arthur worked in one of these sub-camps.

Arthur remained in Ravensbruck until the end of the war, and was liberated there by the Soviet army in May 1945. He returned home to search for family members, most of whom had been killed in concentration camps during the war. He also completed his schooling and studied accounting. While still living in Czechoslovakia, Arthur met and married Gabriela Offenberg, also a survivor of the Holocaust. They went to live in Israel for several years and then, in 1951, they moved to Toronto. They are survived by their two children—one of whom is the author, Kathy Kacer—and two grandchildren.

I WASN'T AFRAID

· Auschwitz, 1944 ·

ANONYMOUS

PEOPLE ASK ME all the time if I was scared—being in the war, losing my parents when I was only sixteen years old, but most of all, being in Auschwitz. You'd think the answer would be, "Yes, of course I was." But believe it or not, it wasn't scary for me. I think I was too naïve to know what was happening to me in Auschwitz, or maybe I just didn't want to know.

When I first found out that my parents and I would be deported there, I thought it was going to be an adventure. You see, I was a small-town girl before the war began, a country bumpkin in many ways. Life in my little town in Hungary always seemed a bit dull and boring. That's probably why I loved visiting Budapest so much. Now *that* was an exciting city, and the girls there always seemed so much more grown up than me. Once a year, my brother, Thomas, and I got on the train to travel to Budapest to visit my grandmother. Whenever I smelled train smoke, I always said, "Now that smells like Budapest," and my anticipation would grow. But other than those infrequent trips, nothing much exciting ever happened. So, I thought the journey to Auschwitz would be an adventure. It turned out to be anything but.

There were horrifying things that happened in the concentration camp—people dying and being killed every day, starvation and disease all around me. The worst moment for me was when I was separated from my parents. My last memory of my mother is watching her walk away from me. She begged the guards not to take her. "*Mein kind,*" she said, pointing to me. "My child." But the guards ignored her pleas. And then she was gone.

"You'll see your mother later," whispered the woman standing next to me. I accepted this lie. You see, I didn't want to believe that my mother was gone for good. But I could not imagine that I *wouldn't* get out alive. For that matter, I didn't imagine that I *would* get out alive. I was neither positive nor negative. I just was.

Auschwitz was a forsaken place—a swampland. There was not a blade of grass anywhere to be seen, no trees, no birds, no life. It was as if God had discarded this land like throwing away a used tissue. But in Auschwitz, I witnessed the most beautiful sunsets I had ever seen. At night, the sun lay low on the horizon, casting a gentle hue of reds and golds—colours that were completely absent by day. I looked forward to those sunsets—couldn't wait until each dreary day had ended and I could gaze upon something that was beautiful. You can forget about beauty in a place like that, just as you can forget about laughter and love. And I didn't want to forget those things.

I kept my sense of humour in Auschwitz—or at least I tried to. The day I arrived, all the girls and women had to give up their dresses, sweaters, coats, and blouses. The only things we were allowed to keep were our shoes. And I was luckier than most. I had a pair of men's shoes that I had been given in the ghetto, where I was imprisoned before. The shoes weren't fashionable, but they were sturdy. In place of our clothing we were given other dresses to wear, those that had been left behind by the Jewish prisoners who had gone before us. The dress that I received was long and green, with a pink satin collar. Can you imagine how ridiculous I looked? There I was, wearing a long, tasteless party gown in the middle of a concentration camp.

You might wonder how things could possibly have

seemed funny in that monstrous place, and believe me, there wasn't a lot to laugh at. But I looked for things that were encouraging, things that kept my spirits high—just like the sunsets, and the ridiculous dress that I wore. I think when you're young you can adjust to almost anything, and I adjusted well. Humans are the most adaptable animals, and the truth is, we simply did not have a choice. We didn't have time to be afraid. We had to adapt, or give up and die. My father always said that you could look at the world as a glass that was half full, or one that was half empty. I chose the glass half full.

The part of Auschwitz in which I was imprisoned held about thirty thousand women, and I was assigned to Block 30—the most disgusting building in the entire camp. If Auschwitz was a forsaken land, then Block 30 was its castoff—worse than revolting. It was the last in a row of barracks, a long, flat wooden structure. A thousand women were crammed into this one barrack. And there were not even bunk beds, just a dirt floor with one long oven that ran the length of the structure. The oven was supposed to provide heat, but naturally, it didn't. We all sat slumped against one another or against the wall.

The Nazis were obsessed with counting Jewish prisoners. Twice a day, we were ordered to assemble outside. "*Heraus!*" the guards yelled. "Everyone out!" And we scrambled in response. We lined up, one behind the other in rows of five, hugging the one in front of us for warmth, while the guards walked among the endless rows of women and added up the number of prisoners—five, ten, fifteen, one hundred, five hundred, one thousand, and so on. Every single one of the thirty thousand women in this camp had to be accounted for. It took a long time to complete the count. But if the total number was off by even one, then the counting went on forever. We stood for hours and hours, and eventually we would be ordered to kneel while the count continued. I tried to stay alert during the count. I tried to think of the sunsets, or the train rides to Budapest. I tried to make up songs in my head—anything that might distract me from what was really happening. Besides, you didn't want to fall down during the count or one of the guards would make it even more unbearable, screaming and beating you.

It was during one of those endless counts that I first spied Agi. Agi was my very best friend from home, a comforting and familiar face in those barren surroundings. I couldn't believe she was there, and I couldn't wait until the count was over so that I could get to her. That day, it seemed to go on longer than ever. Finally we were dismissed, and I scurried among the crowds of women over to where my friend stood.

"Agi!" I cried. "I'm so happy to see you."

Agi stood with her mouth open, speechless at first. The truth is, we barely recognized one another. We were both bald as babies, and even that seemed funny to me. "Julianna," she finally managed to say as we hugged one another in the open yard. "I can't believe it's you."

"You're the first person I've seen from home. I don't know where my parents are," I added. This was always the first item of conversation among prisoners. *Have you seen my aunt, my sister, my uncle?* Prisoners were hungry for crumbs of information suggesting that their loved ones might still be alive. That information was food for our starving souls.

Agi nodded. There was nothing more to say. "I'm lucky," she said. "I'm in Block 29 with my mother." Not only did Agi have her mother with her, but she also had her sister, her cousin, and three other relatives. It was a family all together, and they were steps away from where I was imprisoned all alone.

"We have rows of wooden boards to sleep on in my building," Agi added.

All of the barracks, with the exception of mine, were equipped with these wooden bunks. It didn't matter that these so-called beds were just thin wooden slats on three levels, each one crammed with eight prisoners. If one wanted to roll over, all eight had to shift. None of that mattered. I was sleeping on a dirt floor, while Agi had her family in a building with wooden beds.

"You've got to find a way to move over to our barrack," said Agi.

It was just what I was thinking. But I knew even before I replied that this was going to be impossible.

The Block Elder in Agi's barrack was a woman named Fanny, and her job was to keep order. She was also in charge of counting the prisoners and reporting the numbers to the camp officer. She was the boss, and everyone knew it. The Nazis were clever that way. They made Jewish prisoners control other Jewish prisoners. Sometimes these Block Elders were worse than the Nazi guards themselves. Fanny's helper was a seventeen-year-old prisoner named Dora. If Fanny was the queen of the barracks, then Dora was her sidekick, and the one who did Fanny's dirty work. Dora carried a wooden cane wherever she went, and she wasn't afraid to use it. She was a cruel and heartless young girl who looked for ways to torment the other Jewish prisoners. I didn't hate Dora, though most of the others did. The truth was she had seen her own parents killed by the Nazis and it had driven her crazy. I often wondered, though, how someone with such a sweet face like hers could act like such a wild animal. She was vicious, and no one wanted to get in her way.

"If Dora finds out that I've switched barracks, it will be the end for me," I said.

Prisoners could not switch barracks on a whim, though there was no logical reason why not. It made no difference if one thousand people were crammed into a barracks building, or one thousand and one. It was the total number of prisoners that mattered in the count, not the number per building. But order was the name of the game in Auschwitz. And the Block Elders and their sidekicks needed to believe that they were in charge. Switching barracks would be a blow to their authority and control, and I knew I would pay for it if I were discovered. But in that moment, I didn't care about the consequences. I knew I needed to get to Agi's barrack, no matter what. And there was only one way to do it. In the next count, I would simply slip into Agi's line and hope with all my might that Dora did not notice. If everything went according to plan, the count would be correct, and I would be in Agi's building. I explained the plan to Agi, and she nodded in agreement.

I waited for the next time we were to assemble outside. My heart raced in anticipation. But I wasn't scared. I was the girl who longed for adventure, and this was a new challenge for me—some excitement in the midst of all that dreariness. The minutes and hours ticked by. Normally, I dreaded the approaching count and the time we were made to stand in one place. But that day, it couldn't come fast enough.

As soon as I heard the whistle for roll call, I made my move. I jumped up from the dirt floor in my barrack and headed outside, even before the other women had begun to move. Agi was just across the way, and she lifted her head when she saw me and nodded slightly. I glanced around, looking to see if Dora was anywhere in sight. The coast was clear. Trying to appear as inconspicuous as possible, I slipped out of my line and walked over to where Agi and her family stood. They grabbed me, pushing me into their line as the count began. My heart was beating harder, not from fear, but with exhilaration. It was an adrenaline rush, as if I had defied the odds and done something daring and dangerous all at the same time. This was the kind of excitement that I had longed for. It brought the blood pulsing back into my veins.

The count ended and we were dismissed. Jubilantly, I walked into Block 29 with Agi and her family and made my way over to one of the bunks. "I did it!" I nearly shouted out loud to Agi. "Now as long as I steer clear of Dora, she'll never know what happened." But I had spoken too soon. I was just about to lay my head upon a wooden board when another girl entered the barrack.

"Dora is on her way over here," she said, looking me directly in the eye. "And she's on the warpath."

My heart sank. "She must have seen me sneak over here," I said. "She knows I don't belong." Dora could never tolerate the thought that someone had defied her authority. Now she was coming for me, and who knew what the consequences were going to be.

Agi looked over at me. "What are we going to do?" she asked. She was shaking and her eyes were wide and glassy. She did not want to be implicated in this scheme.

But there was no time for me to reply. The door to the barrack burst open and Dora strode inside. She had eagle eyes, and even in the massive barrack, she spied me immediately.

"Get out!" she screamed. "Get out, now!" Dora looked like a wild dog, hungry for blood. Her body practically shook with rage as she lunged towards me. The two of us began to fight, wrestling with one another as Agi and the other prisoners looked on. Dora had her hands around my neck and I struggled to pull her arms away. I slapped wildly at her face and kicked her hard in the shins. Once again, I was grateful for those sturdy men's shoes of mine.

Dora was strong. She punched hard at my shoulders and back. But I returned her blows with more of my own. I knew what I was doing. I had grown up with an older brother and I knew how to wrestle. I knew that I was not going to be beaten by anyone, including a wild-eyed Jewish girl. No matter how tough she thought she was, I knew I was tougher.

Slowly but surely, I began to get the upper hand. I could feel Dora weakening in front of me. And finally, with a cry of outrage, Dora pulled away and jumped out of my reach. She was breathing heavily, facing me with the same loathing and anger in her eyes, but also something else. She looked defeated.

"I'm going to get my cane!" she wheezed. "And then you'll be sorry."

Dora turned and marched out of the building. For a moment no one moved. Then, a group of women surrounded me, pounding me on the back and shouting out their congratulations.

"She's going to come back," Agi finally said. "We've got to hide you."

I nodded. "I am going to climb into the top bunk," I said firmly, "and hide in the back. She'll never see me there." Quickly, I jumped onto the highest wooden bunk and crawled into the farthest corner. I curled myself into a small round ball and waited. It did not take long. Minutes later, the door to the barrack burst open again. Dora had returned.

"Where is she?" Dora demanded.

I didn't have to see her to know that she would be crazy with anger. No one replied.

"Well then, I'll find her myself," Dora shouted. "And when I do, she will pay." And then, all I could hear were loud footsteps as Dora strode the length of the barrack in her boots. Periodically, the stomping stopped, and I imagined Dora peering into each bunk bed, searching underneath the wooden slats, looking everywhere for her prey. I pushed farther into the corner, hoping to make myself as invisible as possible while the search continued.

Minutes passed. They felt like hours. And then, miraculously, the door to the barrack opened again, and Dora left. I waited a few more minutes, wondering anxiously if this was just a short reprieve. Would Dora come back again looking for me? Finally, I crawled out from the bunk and climbed down to face Agi.

"What if she comes back?" Agi asked, still somewhat anxious.

I shrugged. "I don't think she will. But I'll cross that bridge if I have to."

I stayed with Agi and her family after that. And though I still avoided Dora, somehow I knew that she would not come after me again. I continued to fight for life every day, and I knew I would survive. So you see, that is what Auschwitz was for me. It was not a place where I was afraid. I could see what fear was doing to others in the concentration camp. It was killing them faster than starvation and disease. I was determined not to let that happen to me. I looked fear in the face and I refused to let it get the better of me.

POSTSCRIPT

The names in this story have been changed as the survivor asked not to be identified. She now lives in Montreal.

THE ANGEL
OF DEATH

• Auschwitz-Birkenau, 1944 •

HELLMUTH SZPRYCER'S STORY

Left: *Hellmuth Szprycer as a young boy.* Right: *Hellmuth Szprycer, in an American army uniform, taken a few months after the war ended.*

HE WAS CALLED "the Angel of Death"—Dr. Josef Mengele, the concentration camp doctor. Thirteen-year-old Hellmuth watched him stride through the barrack and wondered silently how such a man could be called a doctor. Doctors were meant to heal the sick and help the weak. This man—this *doctor*—was not a healer. He held the power of life in his hands, but he used that power to inflict pain and death.

Mengele was impressive-looking with his elegant, neatly pressed uniform, shiny boots, and movie-star good looks. *Looks are deceiving*, Hellmuth thought. There was only one reason why Mengele had appeared in the barrack on this day. There was to be a selection. Hellmuth thrust his shoulders back and stared straight ahead as Mengele walked slowly through the centre of the barrack room, carefully inspecting the prisoners. The doctor carried a riding crop in one hand and rhythmically slapped it into the palm of the other. Each boy seemed to shrink back from the sight of the whip, waiting for the blows to fall. But this crop was not to be used to strike the Jewish prisoners, though that might have been a preferred option. The crop was used to indicate which direction each prisoner was to move. "*Links*," left, meant life. Those boys selected would be put to work. "*Rechts*," right, meant the prisoner was destined for death.

Hellmuth had arrived in the Auschwitz-Birkenau concentration camp in September 1943. As soon as he'd entered the gates of the camp, Hellmuth had known that it would take all his cunning and ingenuity to survive there. Auschwitz was a place of extremes—extreme starvation, filth, sickness, and the constant threat of death. But Hellmuth was smart, and resourceful. He was good at sizing up a situation, knowing who to get close to and who to avoid. There were prisoners who tried to remain invisible, tried to pass under the radar of the Nazi soldiers. If they were not noticed, they might be able to avoid danger. But that was not Hellmuth's style. *I will make the Nazi officers pay attention to me*, he said to himself. *That's how I will stay alive.*

Hellmuth realized immediately that there were a few boys his age who seemed to be in privileged positions in the camp. They wore special uniforms and moved in areas of Auschwitz where others could not go. They were known as "*laufers*," or messengers. They did odd jobs for the concentration camp officers—cleaning boots and cars, waiting at the gates for the arrival of each new transport, searching through luggage that had been taken from prisoners upon their arrival. Often, they were paid for their duties with food—and in Auschwitz, food was life.

That's the job for me, thought Hellmuth. *If I'm to survive here, I will become a laufer.*

It wasn't long before Hellmuth received his uniform—a blue jacket and riding boots—and was assigned to clean the motorcycles of the Nazi officers. He would click his heels in salute to the officers as if he were in the army.

"I'll clean your motorcycle at once, *Obersturmführer*," Hellmuth would say in German, addressing the Nazi officer by title. "And if you would like, I will clean your boots as well."

Most of the Nazi officers seemed to like him; perhaps they were amused by him. They must have been impressed with his boldness and strength. And even when some officers, the brutal ones, kicked him, Hellmuth would not show weakness or pain. He got up immediately and continued to work. They called him "*Berliner*"—the smart Jewish boy, born in Berlin, who spoke perfect German.

But no matter how strong or cunning you were, in Auschwitz you could not avoid the selection. Hellmuth was strong and in good physical shape for a boy who had spent the last six months in this death camp. But the selection was a game of chance, a roll of the dice. Everyone was vulnerable, no matter how fit.

Hellmuth glanced again down the length of the barrack waiting to see whom Mengele would choose for life and death. The doctor whistled under his breath as he strode through the building. His cap was tilted almost playfully to one side. He might have been on a leisurely walk, if his purpose had not been so deadly. Hellmuth was struck by the contrast between what Mengele looked like and what he was. He looked like a socialite. But he was a hunter, and the Jewish prisoners were the hunted: cat and mouse; search and destroy. Mengele surveyed his prey calmly with steely dark eyes, and then moved in for the kill.

"*Rechts! Rechts! Links! Links!*" Mengele gave the orders and gestured to each side of the barrack room. Boys moved quickly in response to his command. Those who lined up on the left side of the room gave visible sighs of relief, while those on the right hung their heads and cowered in disbelief.

Hellmuth watched it all and knew he would not wait to discover his own fate. He moved out of line and approached the concentration camp doctor.

Clicking his heels together in salute, Hellmuth stopped directly in front of Mengele. "Don't send me to the gas chamber, *Obersturmbannführer*," Hellmuth said, addressing the doctor by his official rank and title. "I can work for you. I can clean your shoes. I can do anything you want." Hellmuth stood straight and tall, unflinching. And he spoke his best German to this man who had the power to take life, or prolong it.

What nerve! What daring! What would Mengele think? How would he respond to this impudent Jewish boy who dared to stand up to him? Hellmuth could almost hear the gasps from the other boys in the room. Had he sealed his own fate with this bold and reckless gesture?

Mengele stared calmly at Hellmuth, eyeing him up and down. Then the faintest of smiles crossed his lips and he nodded his head briefly. "Okay, *Berliner*. I'll spare your life. *Links!*"

Life! Hellmuth would live—another hour, another day, perhaps another week or month. But he couldn't think too much about the distant future. For now, all that was important was that his life was spared. Hellmuth clicked his heels once more, turned, and began to join the line of boys on the left of the barrack room. But just as he was about to step into the line of prisoners who had also been granted life, Hellmuth was stopped by a young boy.

"Please help me," the boy whispered.

Hellmuth paused and glanced at the boy. How old was he? Twelve? Thirteen? In this place, it was hard to tell. Boys looked like withered old men. This one stood, trembling, in a line of boys who had yet to pass before Mengele. Tears streamed down his pale, gaunt cheeks as he pleaded with Hellmuth.

"I don't know much German," the boy whispered. "I don't want to die." He gestured towards Mengele. "Please, talk to him for me too."

Hellmuth lowered his eyes. *Why should I help this kid?* he wondered. Here in Auschwitz it was hard enough to look after yourself, let alone worry about others. Every man for himself; survival of the fittest; look out for number one. Hellmuth was about to turn away and join his line when something stopped him. Was it the painful, pleading look in this boy's eyes? Was it his helplessness? The boy was small and weak-looking. There was no doubt in Hellmuth's mind that his fate would be sealed when he passed before the doctor.

"Please," the boy begged once more. "My name is Harry."

Hellmuth sighed, realizing that he had no choice but to try and help Harry. *If we don't watch out for one another, then who will watch out for us?* he thought as he turned around to face Mengele once more.

Hellmuth took a deep breath. "I know this boy, *Obersturmbannführer*," he said. "Please, spare his life too."

The doctor's eyes narrowed and he glared as Hellmuth spoke. This was defiance in the face of Mengele's authority. He was no longer amused by Hellmuth's daring. *What have I done?* Hellmuth wondered. *I've forfeited this kid's life, and my own. There will be two more of us dead by this afternoon.* Nevertheless, Hellmuth stood as tall as he could, undaunted in the face of Mengele's growing anger.

A minute passed. No one moved. The entire barrack room had gone silent as everyone watched Mengele and Hellmuth face off against one another. The man with ultimate power and the boy with none at all stared into one another's eyes. Finally, Mengele smiled and motioned for Harry to step forward.

"So," Mengele said slyly, "you want life for your friend too?"

The boys stood side by side silently. Mengele eyed them both and then reached into his uniform pocket. He withdrew a small box of matches, opened it, and pulled out one wooden match. As the boys watched, Mengele broke the match in half and placed both halves between his thumb and forefinger. Then he held up his hand.

"I have two sticks here," he said. "Each of you will pick one. Whoever picks the longer stick will live. The other will die."

Hellmuth took a deep breath. *Why doesn't this Nazi just shoot us both and get this over with?* he thought as he and Harry stepped forward. But the answer was clear. This was entertainment for Mengele. He was playing with the boys, playing with their lives. This was a game of cat and mouse. Who would blink first? Who would win the prize?

Hellmuth refused to show his fear. Standing his ground, he reached up for one of the sticks. Harry, trembling and shaky, did the same. Both boys withdrew sticks and held them up for Mengele to see. Hellmuth held the longer of the two.

With a nod of his head, Mengele motioned the boys back into their places. Hellmuth felt weak with relief and turned to rejoin his line. His life had been spared once more. Harry could not stop himself from crying, and he sobbed uncontrollably as he moved into the line destined for the gas chambers.

As the boys returned to their places, Harry turned to Hellmuth once more. "I beg of you," he pleaded. "Do something to save me."

Hellmuth shook his head and turned away. What more could he do? He had risked his own life to help this boy, and he had failed. There were no more options. Besides, how could he approach Mengele again? Once was daring enough. The second time had nearly gotten him killed. A third time would be like throwing his own life away. Only a fool would take that kind of chance, and Hellmuth was no fool.

Harry reached out and grabbed Hellmuth by the arm. With pleading eyes, Harry implored Hellmuth to do something, anything.

Hellmuth shook his arm free. Why didn't this kid leave him alone? So many "why?"s swirled around inside Hellmuth's head. Why was he—a thirteen-year-old boy— even in the position of having to fight for his life? Why wasn't he off playing soccer, or volleyball, like other thirteen-year-olds, instead of having to play this game of life and death? And why didn't he have his own family there to look after him? Hellmuth had no one except himself. His parents, grandparents, and sisters were all gone. Maybe it was better that way, Hellmuth often thought. No one else to worry about. But often, Hellmuth longed to be sheltered by a family—by people who loved and cared for him. For Hellmuth, the stars that he watched at night became symbols of his family members. "This one is my grandfather, those are my sisters," he would whisper as he gazed at the night sky. "Perhaps they are watching me, as I watch them above me."

"*Please*," Harry whispered once more.

Hellmuth sighed. *Perhaps there is strength in numbers*, he thought as he turned and approached Mengele for the third time. "*Obersturmbannführer*," Hellmuth said, once more drawing himself up to his fullest height. "Give this boy something to do. Make him a *laufer* and he will do his best for you. I know it."

Silence, as Mengele stared at Hellmuth. *What is he thinking?* Hellmuth wondered. There was no charity in this man—no kindness. No one really knew how his evil mind worked. Either he would find Hellmuth's actions gutsy and admirable, or he would dismiss them with a nod of his head. Two more dead Jews meant nothing to one who was called the Angel of Death.

It seemed as if an eternity passed while Hellmuth and Mengele again stood face to face. And then, with the slightest flick of his finger, Mengele motioned for Harry to join the line of those who would live. Harry's life had been spared.

Mengele finished the selection quickly and left the barrack. The boys who were to die followed, their heads hanging low upon their chests.

Once they had left, the room erupted in commotion. Boys hugged one another and returned to their bunks, each one relieved for the moment to be out of danger. Hellmuth felt his body go weak. All he wanted to do was lie down, close his eyes, and try to forget what had just happened. But there was no relief for Hellmuth. How long before another selection? How long before he would have to beg for life once more? How many others would die so that he could continue to live?

A hand touched Hellmuth's shoulder, and he turned to look at Harry. Tears were streaming down Harry's cheeks, and his already-frail body looked as if it would crumple.

"Thank you," Harry said. "Thank you for giving me my life."

Hellmuth shrugged. "I didn't give you your life," he said, as he moved towards his bunk. "I merely asked for it."

POSTSCRIPT

Hellmuth was in Auschwitz from September 1943 until February 1945. He remained somewhat safe because of his position as a messenger for Josef Mengele. Despite his privileged position, conditions for Hellmuth in Auschwitz were harsh. Near the end of the war, the Nazis decided to abandon the concentration camps. Hellmuth and thousands of prisoners were forced on a death march. He survived this as well and was eventually liberated.

After the war, Hellmuth smuggled himself on a boat to England and was reunited there with his mother, the only member of his immediate family to have survived the war. Years later, Hellmuth married. When his wife, Vera, died, Hellmuth married Shoshana, who already had four sons from a previous marriage. Hellmuth became a successful antiques dealer. He and Shoshana live in California.

More than fifty years after the end of the war, Hellmuth was reunited with Harry, the young boy he had helped save in the Auschwitz concentration camp. To read another story about Hellmuth, see "The Whistler" in *Whispers from the Ghettos.*

THE FOUR SELECTIONS

• Auschwitz, 1944 •

ARNOLD FRIEDMAN'S STORY

A drawing of Arnold Friedman as a young boy, about thirteen years old.

Surviving a selection is more than just a brush with death. It is like climbing out of a burning building. It is like already drowning and then being granted a gulp of air. Surviving a selection leaves you weak with relief and wondering how you can go on.

I AM FOURTEEN YEARS OLD and my name is Arnold. I am a teenager—some would say a child. Auschwitz is not a place for children, but no one seems to care about that—certainly not the Nazis who have imprisoned us here, or the world that seems to have forgotten us.

I have been looking for my father but I can't find him. I don't know where my mother is. I don't know where my brothers, Shlomo and Herschel, are. I don't know what has become of my sisters, Baila and Shandi. Their names stir memories. Let me tell you something about my sisters. The name Baila means beautiful in Italian—like the word *bella*. Shandi means beautiful in German—the word is *shaindel*. Both of my sisters have been given names that mean beautiful. Sometimes I think about that and it makes me smile. There is little to smile about here. In Auschwitz, nothing is beautiful except that memory.

The First Selection

Dr. Mengele is coming. It is August 1944, and we have just begun the high holy day of Rosh Hashanah, the Jewish New Year. If I were back in Hungary, I would be going to the synagogue with my family. We would eat sweet foods, like apples dipped in honey. We would listen to the blowing of the *shofar*, the trumpet made from a ram's horn. The sound is meant to awaken the listener to be mindful of the coming judgment. I recite my prayers by heart and am mindful of the dangers that lie ahead.

The barracks *kapo* blows the whistle and we line up as if

we are going to be counted. The Nazis are crazy about counting. Every day, twice a day, we line up in formation and the Nazis begin to count. Ten, twenty, one hundred, one thousand. There are five thousand boys living in these barracks, and every single one must be accounted for. We stand a long time until the count is complete.

But on this day, when the whistle blows, it is not for a count. This time it is something different, and we stand and wait for Mengele to appear. He walks towards the line of boys with two SS soldiers by his side. He carries a riding crop and taps it against his leg as he strolls towards us. He appears cheerful, whistling a tune, but his intention is deadly.

"Remove your shirts!" the *kapos* shout, and that is the signal for the fight for life. Life depends on strength. If you look weak, you will not survive. Quickly, I unbutton my shirt and drop it to the ground. I am shivering even though it is hot. Shirts are dropping all around me as the boys undress and get ready to be inspected.

"First line, move forward!"

Mengele shouts this order and the first line of boys takes a step. Mengele walks down the line, examining each boy carefully, his eyes glancing the full length of their bodies. We are cattle and he is inspecting the herd, looking for flaws and imperfections. No one returns his stare, but no one can look down. Our eyes are focused forward, for Mengele demands that attention.

"You, you, you, line up over there! The others, go there!"

As the line separates, I glance quickly at the boys in each group. Those on one side look thinner, weaker, and smaller than those on the other side. Among them, I can see my cousin, Matyu, and several boys from my hometown. I know instinctively that I must not end up on the side of these weaker boys.

"Second line, step forward!"

It is my turn, and I take a step. There is no time to think or feel, just to act. Mengele is walking past me and I continue to stand at attention, hardly daring to breathe, fixing my eyes on a spot in the distance.

"You, you, you, over there," he shouts. I catch my breath and move towards the stronger boys, and I know that I am on the side of life.

The selection ends, and half the group of boys are marched off while the rest of us put our shirts back on. We are dismissed and move towards the barracks. We do not talk.

I don't want to think too much about what will happen to Matyu and the other boys who are marched away, but I can't shut my mind off. I know all too well that Jews are regularly marched to their death in Auschwitz. The whispers of other prisoners are hard to ignore. I cannot close my eyes to the burning smokestack in the distance.

An older prisoner who is working in the yard looks up. "Wave goodbye to your buddies," he says.

The Second Selection

It is Yom Kippur, the holiest day in the Jewish year. This is a day of prayer, a day to ask forgiveness for past sins. I wonder if any of the guards are asking to be forgiven for what they are doing to us. Yom Kippur is also a day when you must refrain from eating and drinking. The little bit of food we receive each day is life-sustaining, and it is hard to imagine going without, but we decide to fast in honour of this special day. So, I do not eat my breakfast of one slice of stale bread. I carry my bowl of weak coffee and my one piece of bread around with me. I will fast and remember those who have lost their lives.

"Mengele is coming!" someone shouts, and a wave of fear sweeps through the barracks. The Nazis do not care that it is our holy day. They do not care that we are trying to remember our brothers and sisters, our parents, cousins, aunts, and uncles. They have deliberately planned this selection on the most sacred day of the Jewish year. Yom Kippur is instantly forgotten. I stare at the bread in my hand and quickly gulp it down. All around me, the other boys are gulping their bread as well. We must all try to look healthy for the selection.

When it is over, I am safe once more. As the condemned boys are marched away, one looks back and shouts, "Remember the anniversary of our death!" I make a mental note to add them to my prayers if I am lucky enough to be alive on the next Yom Kippur.

The Third Selection

I have become streetwise. I know the rules of this life-and-death game. I have learned how to stand, where to place myself, how to look. But there are fewer and fewer of us left after each selection, so the chance of surviving becomes smaller each time. How many times can you roll the dice and have them fall in your favour?

Today, the guards have decided to do something different. We are marched to a clearing behind the barracks. There are goalposts in this field, and one SS officer has nailed a wooden stick to a post. Everyone will walk under this marker. Only those who are tall enough will make it through this selection.

I am small in stature and know that I am doomed unless I can come up with a plan. I know that I must stall and play for time. So, as the line moves forward towards the marker, I inch my way back. Two groups are forming ahead of me. Tall boys are on one side of the field, and the skinny, smaller boys are on the other. No one has noticed me yet, but time is running out. Soon I will be at the head of the line and it will be my turn to pass under the wooden stick.

"Get back in the line!" a *kapo* shouts as, once more, I sneak backward.

"I just want to be with my brother at the end," I lie.

He shrugs and moves away. But I am not safe yet. There are only twenty boys left to pass under the marker and I am one of them.

Suddenly, the back of the line where I am standing begins to weave out of its straight formation. We sway towards the group of tall boys who have been granted life, and I realize that this is the chance I have been waiting for. When no one is watching, I jump over and into the safe group and am instantly dwarfed by the boys around me. There are two bricks lying on the ground, and I jump onto them, trying to look tall. For a moment, I think I am safe. For an instant, I believe that I have fooled the guards once more—that I have cheated death. But that moment disappears when a *kapo* grabs me by the back of my prison uniform.

"What do you think you are doing?" he shouts.

He is about to throw me into the other group. He is about to seal my fate, when suddenly I duck away from him. I dive into the group of tall boys and crouch down so no one will see me. Just then, someone blows a whistle, ordering the *kapos* to line up and move off. Through the throng of boys who have surrounded me, I can see this *kapo* searching the crowd, trying to spot me in the forest of tall boys who are jostling together. A moment later, he abandons his search. He and the other *kapos* form a human chain around the group of condemned boys, who are marched away.

The Fourth Selection

It is September 1944, and I have learned that my father is still alive and is here in Auschwitz. I do not know where he is or if I will see him, but just knowing that he is alive gives me new hope. I no longer feel completely alone, and I am filled with memories of home—of going to the synagogue twice a day with my Tatte and watching him bend and sway as he recites his prayers. I try to cling to these memories—to hold on to them like a drowning swimmer clutching a life raft. But it is nearly impossible to keep memories alive. They are daydreams against a backdrop of despair.

There are not many of us left in my barrack. Several more weeks have passed, and we remaining boys are rounded up and marched out to the gate again. There, a guard counts us before opening the gate to let us out. Germans carrying machine guns surround us, and a soft murmur goes through the lines as we realize that this might be the end for all of us. There can be only one reason for our being led out of the concentration camp. There can be only one reason for the guards to carry their guns. We will march out of the gate and to the gas chamber. This is the end of the line, and we know it.

"They must know what is going on," a guard says, surprised that we are so calm in the face of impending death.

The truth is that not one of us wants to die. I want to live. I am young and deserve a future. But I wonder if I will have one. I barely have a present. And so, we march quietly towards whatever is in store.

We are just about to pass under the gate when suddenly a high-ranking officer appears. He is dressed in an impressive uniform with gold braids that bounce across his chest as he approaches.

"Where are you taking these boys?" he demands. "There are healthy-looking ones here who can still work."

"We have been given orders—" a guard begins to reply, but he is instantly cut off.

"Bring them back to the barracks," the officer commands.

We turn and march back to the nearest empty block. The barrack is a long wooden building that houses hundreds of us on wooden bunks that are stacked three tiers high. A chimney-like pipe that runs along the middle of the floor, from one end of the building to the other, is meant to provide heat but gives little. It is here in this barrack, we now understand, that we will have the selection.

The officer stands in the middle of the long room and orders some boys to step forward.

"Jump over!" he says.

One by one, the healthier boys are ordered to jump over the chimney that divides the building in half. Once they have cleared the large, round pipe, their lives will be spared. The weaker boys are ordered to the back of the barrack.

This is a new game and I am watching carefully. My mind is taking it all in, still thinking, still plotting what I will do next. I have learned that life and death are moments of intuition, and my instinct has become sharp. My goal is to get to the other side of the pipe, and to do it as quickly as possible.

A young boy stands in front of me, no older than ten years of age. He is probably the youngest in the group.

"How old are you?" the officer asks the boy.

"I'm sixteen," he replies. He has also learned something in the fight to survive. Young children are not wanted here. This will be an important exchange, and I am standing behind the boy, listening, and anticipating a moment when I might make my move.

"I said, how old are you?" The officer is not easily fooled.

The boy is shaky and silent, and so I step forward and answer on his behalf. "He says he is sixteen." My voice is strong and clear.

The officer pauses and stares, first at the young boy, and then at me.

"Jump over the pipe," he finally says, and once again, I know that my moment has come.

The boy clears the pipe easily, and as the officer turns slightly to address another boy, I make my move. I spread my arms and leap into the air. I fly across the pipe in the centre of the room. I jump to the other side. I jump towards life.

POSTSCRIPT

When Arnold found out that his father was still alive in Auschwitz, he also learned that he was part of a group of prisoners called the *Sonderkommando*. These prisoners worked in the crematoria of the concentration camps removing bodies from the gas chambers. They were not permitted to have any contact with other prisoners, in case they gave out information about the fate of Jewish prisoners.

Arnold remained in Auschwitz until January 1945, when he and the other prisoners were marched to another concentration camp called Gross-Rosen. From there, he was taken to another camp, called Dachau, and he was finally liberated there by the American army at the end of the war. Eventually, Arnold made his way back to his hometown of Rakosin, which is now part of Ukraine. He searched there for family members, most of whom had perished in the concentration camps.

Arnold went to England in 1946, and came to Canada and to Toronto in 1947. He is married and has two children and five grandchildren.

REMEMBERING
THE HOLOCAUST

• Dachau, 1945 •

GEORGE SCOTT'S STORY

The liberation of Dachau by U.S. soldiers, April 1944. George is second from the left in the front row. Credit: United States Holocaust Memorial Museum

My name is George Scott.

I am a Hungarian Jew.

I don't want to tell you everything,

I don't want to make you sad.

My father died when I was a year old.

My mother died when I was four.

I went to a Jewish orphanage.

They were good to me.

The Nazis stomped into Hungary in 1944.

"*Yazda! Yazda! Yazda!*"

"Move it! Move it! Move it!"

The Nazis were in a hurry to murder Jews.

"*Du affe.*"

A young German solider called me an ape.

"He doesn't look Jewish."

People at the train station turned their backs.

Cattle car.

Three days.

A patch of blue through a wire window.

I know the world out there, but what world is this?

I was fourteen when I arrived in Birkenau, part of
Auschwitz.

He was a small man.

He wore white gloves.

He was Dr. Josef Mengele, and he said I could live a little
while longer.

Hunger hurts before it numbs.
Terrified, truncated, stunned.
Those of us who are still around
Brutes and brutalized, blended into one.[4]

Another selection.
This time I would die.
Then, another man took my place.
He died, I lived.

The gas chamber's red brick chimney burning.
Bald, shaven women, striped like us,
Mothers, daughters, starved, faded, beyond reach.
Rats the size of small dogs.[5]

Another selection.
This time to the kitchen.
Food enough to keep me hungry.
Starving people still breathe.

This is my picture.
Behind barbed wire, in prisoner's uniform,

[4, 5]A stanza from an original poem by George Scott.

Liberated,
Smiling at the Americans and their cameras.

I want you to know,
That I do not hate Germans.
It was only a rotten few.
That I do not hate anyone.

I want you to know
That I believe in God,
That I believe in mankind,
and that I trust a good heart.

POSTSCRIPT

George Scott was born in Budapest in 1930. After the death of his parents, his education continued in the Budapest Jewish Orphanage. In 1944 the Germans occupied Hungary. Attempts to run away from the Nazis failed. George was on the last transport from Hungary to Birkenau. He was transferred to Landsberg in January 1945, and was liberated in Dachau just before his fifteenth birthday.

George arrived in Canada in 1948, married a Scottish girl in Toronto in 1954, and together they had three children. Ruth, the mother of his children, died at age forty-one. He is an unpublished poet, now married to Harriet Brav-Baum, a graphic artist.

FIGHTING FOR LIFE

· Gleiwitz (a sub-camp of Auschwitz), 1944 ·
GEORGE BRADY'S STORY

George Brady as a young boy.
(This photograph is part of the Brady family collection.)

September 29, 1944

The door to the train slid open and George was instantly bombarded with sounds and sights. Floodlights beamed across the faces of the Jewish men standing behind him. Nazi guards screamed orders, while their dogs strained against their leashes and barked ferociously. George blinked and shielded his eyes. He was numb from having travelled a day and a half with no food, locked into this boxcar, practically suffocating in the congestion of too many people crammed into one small space. For a moment, he was disoriented, and then George took his first look at the Auschwitz concentration camp. Confusion was everywhere as the guards continued to shout orders and the prisoners stood in a state of shock.

A group of inmates appeared out of nowhere and jumped up onto the train. "Get out! Get out now!" they shouted as they shoved and pushed George and the others out of the boxcar.

"What about our luggage?" someone asked.

"You'll get it later," a prisoner replied. These prisoners were intent on one thing, and one thing only—to get the Jewish passengers off the train.

"Now move—quickly!"

A mountain of suitcases was beginning to form on the platform. The suitcases were being tossed carelessly onto the growing pile, discarded and neglected. George wondered if he'd ever see his belongings again.

His introduction to Auschwitz was a selection. George lined up with the other prisoners, taking careful note of what was happening up ahead. At the front of the line, a Nazi officer inspected each prisoner, and then the line was divided. Some men and women moved to the left, others to the right.

"Say that you're healthy," someone whispered in George's ear.

The Nazi officer at the front of the line had cool, detached eyes. George passed in front of him, pulling himself up as straight and strong as he could. "*Gesund*," he said quickly in adequate German. "I'm healthy."

With a slight flick of his riding crop, the officer gestured to the right, and George responded quickly. Several people, including two of George's friends, were sent to the left, and George glanced in their direction, wondering what all of this meant. Those on the left appeared weaker than those on the right. George didn't know it at the time, but those on the left were going straight to their death. *Perhaps they are going to do lighter labour*, he thought briefly before the guards shouted once more and the lines moved forward.

It was dark, and George shivered uncontrollably in the cool fall air. The prisoners were marched quickly towards a large warehouse, through a street with barbed-wire fences on either side and rows of barracks just beyond. The wind shifted and George caught a whiff of something vile in the air—smells coming from a distant smokestack. There was no time to think as he and the others were ushered into a building. First, his head was shaved. Next came the showers, and finally prison uniforms. George gasped as he caught a glimpse of himself in a window. He was as bald as a newborn baby. Once he had been a young, strong boy with thick dark hair and a warm, innocent smile. But that seemed so long ago, before the war, before his grandmother, parents, and sister had been taken from him, before he'd been forced to give up his youth. Now George no longer looked like a boy, and he was overcome with fear that life did not exist in this place. *I won't let death come looking for me*, George vowed then and there. But at the age of sixteen, it would be hard to be a hero with death staring him in the face.

October 3, 1944

George and a group of prisoners found themselves being pushed towards a large warehouse. George entered and looked around. Each of the four corners of this building had a sign beckoning the prisoners to come forward. One was marked "Ironworkers," another said "Carpenters," and the third was marked "Labourers." George walked towards the fourth corner and a sign labelled "Youth."

"How old are you?" The man interrogating him was a prisoner, just like George, assigned to work there on behalf of the Nazi guards. These prisoners could speak the many languages of those who were just arriving: Hungarian, Czech, French, Polish.

"I'm sixteen," George replied in a strong voice. Appearing healthy had already saved his life once. Perhaps it would help again.

The man eyed George carefully, stepped forward, and with no warning, slapped him hard across the face! "How old are you?" he demanded again.

George recoiled from the sting. His cheek burned. "I'm sixteen, sir," he replied even more politely than before. And once more, the man stepped forward and slapped him.

Over and over the scene continued; it was like rewinding a movie reel and watching it repeat. George's mind was spinning. He couldn't understand what this man wanted, and he wouldn't give him the pleasure of seeing him break down. George bit his lip and swallowed hard. *Think!* he commanded himself. *Stay calm and think!*

"Tell him you're eighteen," someone behind George said.

One last time the prisoner moved towards George. He lowered his voice and growled, "How old are you?"

George stared into his eyes, searching for an answer—the right answer. Then he took a deep breath and replied, "I'm eighteen years old."

The man paused, nodded, and stepped back.

Just then, an SS man bellowed from across the room. "We need three hundred ironworkers over here." Quickly, George stepped towards him. "I'm an ironworker," he said. The truth was that George was not really trained in ironwork. However, he did have experience as a plumber, a skill he had learned while in Terezin, the place where he had previously been imprisoned. *Tools are tools,* George thought, *and work is a good thing.*

"How old are you?" the man demanded.

"I'm eighteen," George replied. He was not going to fall into that trap again.

"*Zu jung!*" the SS man snapped in German. "Too young!"

George was dismayed, but once again his instincts took over. Something told him that this was the right line, the best choice, the safest place to be in this dangerous situation. He stepped back and off to one side, keeping his eyes and ears open, waiting for just the right opportunity. Other prisoners were gathered at the table, pressing forward to be picked as ironworkers. This was George's chance. When no one was looking, he jumped into the crowd of those chosen to work. *That makes two*, he thought. Two life-and-death moments, two strokes of luck.

George and the other workers were loaded onto another train and taken to Gleiwitz, a sub-camp of Auschwitz. It was a short train ride away, fifty-five kilometres northwest of Auschwitz. George glanced out the small window as the train swayed and rattled towards its new destination. He did not know what harsh conditions lay ahead of him. But he did know that he was leaving certain death behind, and that alone was a reassuring thought.

"George!" Someone grabbed him from behind, and George turned to find his good friend Eda standing behind him.

"Eda! I'm so glad to see someone I know." A familiar face in these alien surroundings was a gift. Eda had also come from Terezin. "Do you know anything about where we're going?" asked George.

Eda shook his head. "Not much," he replied. "I overhead some of the other prisoners. They say we'll be repairing bombed-out railway cars."

"*Ruhe!* Quiet!" The Nazi commands silenced George's conversation. He and the other prisoners had reached their destination. They were herded off the train and lined up to march to their new barracks.

January 17, 1945

Four months passed—four months of unbearable living conditions and brutal labour. The prisoners worked over ten hours a day, seven days a week, replacing and repairing damaged, bombed-out parts of railway cars. It was back-breaking and treacherous work. The only break was the daily lineup for food, if you could call it that. Each prisoner received 800 grams of bread and a watery liquid that was flavourless and lukewarm. For lunch, there was tasteless turnip soup. George had one prison uniform that he could never change or clean, and lice and their accompanying diseases were a constant threat.

Each day, the prisoners were lined up in formation to make the trek over to their worksite. George and the others stood five in a line, arms linked. Twenty lines of five added up to one hundred people, and so on. In this way, the Nazis could easily count the prisoners. And in this formation, it was impossible to think of escaping. An absent prisoner would be easily and immediately noticed. Not that George could even have imagined the possibility of running away.

The only escape for George was in his mind, where his thoughts would wander to other times and other places. He remembered his home in Czechoslovakia, and the happy times he had spent there as a child. He thought about his family's garden, where he and his sister, Hana, had played hide-and-seek together. He recalled skiing in the mountains on family holidays and the joy of building a snow fort. And on top of all of those tender memories he thought about food! When you are starving, food is the only thing on your mind, and George thought about it night and day.

"What I wouldn't give for a steaming *bramboravá polévka*—potato soup," George muttered to Eda one day in the work line.

"I'm dreaming of *knedliky*," Eda replied. "Dumplings! I used to make the best potato dumplings. Or better yet, the sweet ones filled with blueberries." Eda had been a cook by profession. George couldn't tell whether it was helpful to dream about food, or whether it only added to the torture.

It was now the middle of winter and the barrack, with its leaky roof and constant dampness, was also bitterly cold, with an iciness that cut through George's flimsy prison garb straight to his bones. *Is this really better than death?* George sometimes wondered. *Perhaps it would be better to just give up.* But something kept George going, kept him fighting for life. Perhaps it was hope that he would be reunited with his family. Maybe it was a belief that conditions would eventually get better. And perhaps it was just George's personality. He was someone who had never given up on anything, someone who was clever and resourceful and could overcome any hardship. So, George worked and watched. He kept to himself, except for his friendship with Eda.

"Look up there," George muttered to Eda one Sunday. Up above, a lone airplane was flying low over the prison camp. As it passed overhead, George could make out the insignia on the wings. He was startled to realize that the plane was Soviet.

"I've seen the same plane each Sunday for the last few weeks," George continued. "A Soviet plane! Why is it flying so close? And why aren't the Nazis shooting it down?"

Eda paused in his work, looking around quickly to see if the guards were watching. "I think it's the end for the Nazis," he whispered. "Haven't you heard the other prisoners talking? The Soviet Red Army is closing in. Hitler's troops are in trouble. That's the only reason they aren't shooting at the plane. They don't have an air force left to send up and knock this plane out of the sky. Don't you see, George? It could mean the end of the war!" Eda's eyes shone with a brightness and passion that George hadn't seen in a very long time.

George returned to his work. He couldn't dare to imagine that the war might be nearing its end. It was dangerous to think too far into the future. Here in Gleiwitz, life was measured in minutes. Getting through each hour, each day was as far as George would allow his mind to wander.

But on that day in January, George and the others were suddenly ordered to return to their barracks, where they were greeted with a new set of commands.

"Line up in formation," the Nazi guards shouted.

Whispers and bits of conversation were passing through the ranks of the prisoners.

"The Soviets are increasing their offensive. Hitler's armies are retreating," someone said.

"We're leaving," another whispered.

"They are opening the gates. We're being marched out of here."

Everywhere, the whispers were growing louder and more animated. And the word on everyone's lips was evacuation.

George sought out Eda in the crowd. "Where are we going?" he asked. Eda shook his head. No one knew the answer to that question.

As the prisoners were being assembled, each one was given a loaf of bread. At first glance, it seemed like a feast! But that feeling didn't last.

"This is all the food you'll have for the next ten days," the Nazi guards warned. "So use it wisely."

George lifted the loaf to his nose and inhaled. The temptation to eat the bread immediately was overwhelming.

But George knew he had to resist the urge to stuff it into his mouth, so instead he stuffed it into his shirt.

When everyone was accounted for, the gates to Gleiwitz opened and George and seven hundred fellow prisoners began to march out of the prison camp.

January 20, 1945

The march lasted for three days. That first day, the prisoners walked and walked and walked, never stopping to rest. Those who were too weak and couldn't keep up fell to the back of the group and were shot on the spot. Gunshots crackled all around George. Several prisoners lost their minds, ranting and crying out and refusing to take another step. They, too, were left to die in the snow while the rest of the group marched on. Finally, when George thought he could walk no more, the prisoners were told to stop. He sank to the ground in the dimming light, exhausted, starving, and cold.

The trees by the side of the road were strangely beautiful, with snow hanging heavily from their limbs. In the distance, George could make out lights from some small cottages in the clearing. *Inside those homes, people are warm, and fed, and safe,* he thought. *And we are here, being marched to death. What did we possibly do to deserve this?*

On the second day of the march, George and the others were forced to cross the Oder River. They marched across the bridge with the ever-present Nazi guards prodding them along with their guns and threats. But the next day, the prisoners were turned around and ordered to cross back. Once again, George could not know how lucky this turn of events was. By crossing back across the Oder River, George and the other prisoners ended up on the side that was no longer under Nazi control.

"Don't you see?" whispered Eda, who had remained at George's side throughout the march. "The guards are totally confused. They don't know which way to march us. It's a good sign. The Red Army must be nearby. Stay strong."

George nodded. He wanted to believe that this was a good omen. He wanted to hope for rescue. But he was numb. The only thing he could think of was placing one foot in front of the other and not falling behind.

Finally, on the third day of the march, George and the others approached the gates of a new prison camp. The sign above the opening said Blechhammer.

A concrete wall topped with barbed wire surrounded the Blechhammer prisoner-of-war camp. This was not new to George. In fact, Blechhammer looked like every other prison camp he had been in—with one important exception. Blechhammer had hot running water, a luxury! *This is heaven*, thought George, suddenly forgetting his hunger and fatigue. *Not only will I be able to shower, but I'll be able to do it in hot water.*

Happily, almost giddily, the prisoners ran for their showers. But there was one problem facing George—what to do with his precious remaining bread. "I can't hold it in the shower, and I won't leave it here to be stolen by someone else," George said to Eda. The two young men stared at one another, until suddenly another prisoner approached them. Tuli was his name.

"I'll tell you what," Tuli said, "I'll watch your bread while you shower, and then you can watch mine."

George nodded, stripped down, and dove under the hot running water. Never had anything felt so good. *When was the last time I had a hot shower?* he wondered. He couldn't remember. He leaned into the shower, letting the hot water pour across his body, rinsing away the months of grime and filth. All too soon, the shower ended. George dressed quickly and went to find his friend who had been guarding the bread. But to George's dismay, Tuli was fast asleep, and the bread was nowhere in sight.

"Wake up!" George shook Tuli harshly. "What have you done? Where is the bread?"

Startled, Tuli jumped up and glanced around. "Oh no," he cried. "I only fell asleep for a minute. But someone must have stolen my bread and yours."

George was desperate. He had finally had the shower he'd longed for, but now he had no food. How was he going to survive until the next rations were distributed?

January 22, 1945

Blechhammer camp was a place of complete chaos. Nazi guards ran back and forth shouting orders, only to retract them in the next instant. They would position themselves in the watchtowers and then suddenly disappear, leaving the towers empty and unsupervised. Prisoners ran in all directions trying to get away from the guards. No one knew what was happening. There was only mayhem.

"What's going to happen to us?" George asked Eda as the two young men huddled in one of the barracks.

Eda shook his head, but had no time to reply. Just then, a violent explosion ripped through the barrack next door, shaking the floor and vibrating the bunks where George and Eda sat.

"They're killing the prisoners!" someone shouted. "They're throwing grenades into the barracks!"

It was clear that the Red Army was approaching, and the Nazi guards did not want to be there when the Soviets arrived. They would need to evacuate Blechhammer soon. But this time, the Nazis did not want to take Jewish prisoners with them. It would be easier to kill the Jews in Blechhammer than to herd them through the open roads and fields, slowing down the Nazi retreat.

"Eda, get outside!" George shouted. "We'll be killed in here!" George and Eda bolted for the door, along with hundreds of other prisoners.

Another loud whooshing sound came and a cannon blasted close to George. As the smoke cleared, he lifted his head and saw a large, gaping hole in the concrete wall surrounding the prison camp. This was his chance.

"Eda!" he shouted. "We're making a break for it. Follow me!"

Without a moment's hesitation, George, Eda, and several other prisoners sprinted for the open hole and ran for their lives. With each step away from Blechhammer, George knew that he was leaving death behind. But at the same time, he and the others did not feel safe. The escapees knew that Nazi troops would be moving along the roads. Any moment, George expected to hear the crack of a rifle and feel the sting of a bullet.

And so, the group moved into the forest, where they hoped that the undergrowth and thick brush would protect them. Snow was falling heavily, making it difficult to run. In his flimsy prison uniform, George's body shook with fear and cold. He stumbled and quickly regained his footing. With each step, George felt the rocks and branches cut into his feet. His boots had huge holes and a thin sole. But none of that mattered. The group had to move, and move quickly.

They hiked for about four kilometres through the thick forest, saying little to one another, staying together, and heading for what they hoped would be safety. George stayed close to Eda. The two of them had been through so much together, and now they needed their mutual strength more than ever.

Finally, after what felt like an endless hike, the group emerged into a small German village. And only then did they stop running.

"Where are we?" George asked, breathing heavily.

"The sign says Ehrenforst," Eda whispered.

There was an eerie silence in this small village. No one walked on the road. No dogs came out to inspect the newcomers. The houses stood empty, with their doors and windows wide open as if the inhabitants had left quickly. The village was completely deserted. All the villagers had fled.

"What do we do now?" Eda asked.

George turned to face his friend and replied firmly, "We find food."

George pushed open the door of the first house and walked inside. The silence was haunting—peaceful and ghostly at the same time. It was strange to enter a deserted house. But George was on a mission. He headed straight for the kitchen and was thrilled to find food still on the table. George snatched at a loaf of bread and a piece of cheese. He stuffed tomatoes and salami into his mouth until he could eat no more. Then, he wandered into the back of the house and into a small bedroom. He wanted clothing. He wanted to strip off his prison uniform, to rid himself once and for all of the trappings of captivity and oppression. His uniform fell at his feet, and in its place, George put on a jacket, riding pants, and high rubber boots. As George turned around, he caught a glimpse of himself in the mirror on the dresser. His face was thin and gaunt—not the face of a young boy.

George thought back over the lucky moments he had had in the past months: making it through the first selection in Auschwitz, becoming an ironworker, surviving the march, escaping from Blechhammer. Without even knowing it at the time, each choice he had made, each timely event, every step in his journey had brought him one step closer to this moment. Standing there in real clothes, with food in his belly, George finally knew that he was free.

POSTSCRIPT

The Soviet army passed through Ehrenforst and officially liberated George on January 26, 1945. He remained in barracks close to the village of Ehrenforst for about one month. At that point, he was ordered to go to Katowitz. Czech nationals like George were being assembled there and put on a train.

For ten days, George travelled through Poland and Ukraine, finally ending up in Eastern Slovakia. Several weeks later, George celebrated the official end of the war in Budapest. He reached his hometown of Nové Mesto one week after the war ended.

In the fall of 1945, George moved to Prague and spent the next four years going to school. He also searched for family members, hoping to find others who might have survived the war. None of his immediate family had survived. In January 1951, George arrived in Canada. Three years later, he opened a plumbing company in Toronto with another survivor of the Holocaust. George married and has four children and seven grandchildren. His story is also told in Karen Levine's book *Hana's Suitcase* (Second Story Press).

MARCH TO FREEDOM

· Flossenburg, 1945 ·

JOHN FREUND'S STORY

John Freund at the age of eleven.

April 10, 1945

We are leaving Flossenburg. We've just received word that all the remaining prisoners in this concentration camp are to be marched out of here. The rumours of Nazi Germany's impending military defeat have been spreading through the camp like wildfire. We don't know why we are leaving Flossenburg. Is it because the Nazis know they are losing the war and they don't want to leave us behind as evidence of their brutality? Or will they take us to a new location and kill all of us there?

"Have you heard?" a prisoner whispers. "The Soviet armies are advancing from the east."

"Yes," another one adds hoarsely. "And the Allies are pushing from the west. Hitler is being squeezed in the middle. It will be over soon. The war will be over and we'll be free."

Free, I think as I join the lines and walk out the gates of this concentration camp, surrounded by more than six hundred prisoners and dozens of Nazi guards. After more than a year in Auschwitz, and two months in Flossenburg, I can't remember what freedom feels like.

April 11, 1945

It is the first day and we have walked over thirty kilometres. If you are fit and healthy, then thirty kilometres is a challenge, but it can be done. I am fourteen years old, and weak and starving. This feels like a death sentence—a death march. I place one foot in front of the other and walk, my head bent against the wind and rain. One step, ten steps, one thousand steps. We are an ant colony crawling across the country.

All around me, my fellow prisoners are falling. They stagger and then collapse by the side of the road, breathing heavily. There they remain as the rest of us continue to move forward. They will die in the dirt, or be shot where they lie. We are ordered to halt while several prisoners bury the dead. No one says prayers for them. I step over their graves and continue walking, all the while hoping that I will not be the next to fall and die.

Stay near the front of the pack, I tell myself. It's the only way to stay alive. If you are near the back, the Nazi soldiers will shoot you. Their guns are everywhere, trained on us as we walk, taunting us, daring us to hesitate, to fall behind. *I won't be among the dead*, I vow to myself. But why do I want to live so desperately? What is there to live for now? Once, my life was simple and untroubled. Scoring a goal in a soccer game was what I longed for—that and riding my bicycle, or playing table tennis with my best friend. An eternity has passed since then. My family has disappeared. My parents are gone, along with my older brother, grandparents, aunts, uncles, cousins, and countless friends. All dead, in this senseless war that has singled out Jews for extermination. I am alone, but still, I want to live. And so, I continue to walk.

April 16, 1945

I have been walking for five days and the march continues. In these past days, hundreds of my fellow Jews have died or been killed. I watched a group of prisoners try to escape today. Ten people made a break for the woods beyond the road. At first, I could not believe their daring, or the strength that they had somehow managed to preserve for this effort. They timed their getaway well, waiting for dusk, when their shadowy figures might not be noticed. I found myself cheering them on as if I were watching a race. *Run*, I silently prayed. *Run as fast as you can. Be the first to the forest and you'll win the prize. Your reward will be life!* But even as I urged the runners on, a shot rang out from behind me, and then five more quickly followed as the guards took aim. Six of the escapees fell in their tracks. Four made it to the woods and disappeared into the safety of the forest.

April 18, 1945

We walked through a village today. The villagers were nowhere to be seen. They had all disappeared behind their locked doors and closed curtains. Were they too afraid to come outside? Or were they ashamed to see how we were being treated?

Some nights we get to sleep in a barn, where the straw provides warmth and some comfort. But tonight I am sleeping in a ditch by the side of the road. The cold, hard ground is still heaven to my weary body. I could probably sleep on nails, glass, or spikes.

I have not eaten in days. The Nazi guards are not concerned with feeding us. Starvation is another way to thin the ranks of the living. I make do with roots and leaves that I snatch from the fields. And I drink the rainwater from the puddles around me. But tonight, when no one is looking, I sneak into a nearby farmer's field. It is a daring and dangerous mission. Hunger will drive a person to do things he would not normally do. The ground is soft in this early spring. I claw eagerly at the earth, scraping away layer after layer of dirt until, finally, I uncover my prize—a potato. It is early in the season and the potato is not fully mature, but I hardly notice. This is food—manna from heaven. I grab the potato, brush the dirt away, and gnaw hungrily. I dig farther and uncover several more. These I shove into my pocket. They will be my nourishment in the days ahead.

April 20, 1945

Today, we are loaded onto open coal cars and, pulled by an old steam engine, we are transported farther across the country. We are travelling west across Germany, and I struggle and push my way to the side of the train car so I can look over the wooden slats at the countryside. The landscape resembles my home country of Czechoslovakia, and I imagine the towns and cities I once knew so well—Prague, Brno, Krumlov—places that I have not seen in the three years since I was sent from home into the concentration camps. I close my eyes and I can see my house, see my school. But the images blur and fade. And when I open my eyes, I am surrounded once again, not by familiar memories, but by sickness, death, and the endless journey.

I fall asleep, rocked by the rhythm of the train. I have learned to sleep standing up, leaning slightly against the wall of the car and the prisoner next to me. It is a fitful sleep, broken by coughs and groans from my fellow prisoners. But today there is another sound that interrupts my slumber. Airplanes are flying overhead, and the drone of their engines grows louder and more ominous with each minute. As the planes swoop close to the trains that transport Jews across Europe, they suddenly let fly with a volley of machine-gun bullets that strike the entire length of the train. The engine screeches to a halt and we dive over the side of the open cars and underneath, onto the railway tracks, huddling together for protection. The airplanes are British and they are closing in on Hitler and his armies, destroying everything in their path in an effort to end the war. Silently I cheer them on, while at the same time praying that I will not be killed in this attack. The irony does not escape me: I might die at the hands of those who have come to rescue me.

A boy my age is screaming and I raise my head to stare at him. He has been hit in the leg by a bullet. His father is holding him in his arms, rocking him back and forth, trying to shield the boy's body with his own. "Help him," the father begs those of us who are hiding under the train next to him. I reach into my pocket and pull out some strips of cloth. I don't even know why I am carrying the rags, but I pass them to the father, who wraps his son's leg and smiles gratefully at me. I wonder what will happen to this boy. Will he live? Will he continue on the march?

Minutes later, the airplane assault is over. Nazi guards appear and force us back onto the trains. Several prisoners are shot trying to escape.

April 22, 1945

We are walking again, and today, one of my fellow prisoners approaches me and tells me he is a palm reader. "Let me look at your hand," he says. "I can tell your future."

Do any of us have a future? I wonder as I open my hand, rub it against my leg to clean the dirt off, and then thrust it forward into the man's grasp.

He eyes my open hand, slowly and carefully tracing a deep line that runs the length of my palm. Several minutes pass while he considers the grooves and furrows, and then he murmurs something underneath his breath. Finally, he looks up, nodding approvingly. "It's good," he says. "You're going to survive."

As the man walks away, I feel my spirits lift. For the first time in as long as I can remember, I feel hopeful. I have no idea who this stranger is, but he has momentarily transformed the bleakness of my life and provided me with a source of energy and inspiration. In that moment, I realize the importance of hope, for without hope, there is no life. So, I cling to this moment of optimism like a drowning man clutching at a rescuer's outstretched arm. And I hang on with all my might.

April 24, 1945

It is raining. A dense fog encircles me, and a steady downpour makes the muddy road underneath my feet thick and treacherous. It has been two weeks since this march began, but it may as well have been two months, or two years. Each footstep is a second, and that is all that is important now. Sixty steps and a minute passes. Three thousand, six hundred steps and an hour goes by. Days blend in this way.

There are probably only two hundred of us left in this group—two hundred marching prisoners, and the armed Nazi guards who always surround us. But today, as I pick my way through the mud, bathed in cooling raindrops, I notice the guards drop back behind our ranks. They appear nervous and agitated, and suddenly they turn on their heels and disappear, running into the forest, leaving us alone and unguarded.

I look around in confusion. Where have the guards gone? Why have they left us alone?

A moment later, as we emerge into a small clearing, there is a strange and frightening sight ahead. A long line of army tanks is approaching, charging forward at great speed. My fellow prisoners and I look at one another frantically. These might be German tanks, withdrawing from the front. Surely they will kill anyone and anything in their path.

"Run!" someone shouts. "Run for your life!"

I do not need a second warning. Turning, I begin to run for cover, dragging my aching legs. My feet are like lead weights and my sprint is slow and laboured. I wonder if I will be shot in the back, and I brace myself for the bullets that I believe will follow. But nothing happens, and cautiously I glance over my shoulder at the approaching tanks. As I do, I see a soldier emerge from a turret. He waves and shouts in my direction, stopping me in my path. It is only then that I see the large silver star emblazoned on each tank. These are Americans. We have been saved!

I turn and walk towards one of the American tanks, towards one of my rescuers. A young soldier sees me approach and leans over the tank to lift me up next to him. He reaches into his pocket and pulls out a chocolate bar, which he offers to me. I stare at the candy, still refusing to believe that I am alive, unable to comprehend that the war is truly over and I am safe. Tears are streaming down my face— the first tears I have allowed myself in years. I wipe them away with the back of my hand. Then, I reach into my pocket and pull out the last raw potato that I have saved. I toss it onto the ground, smile at the American soldier, and reach for the chocolate.

POSTSCRIPT

John survived the death march and was liberated by American soldiers on April 24, 1945. He returned to his hometown in Czechoslovakia to go back to school and search for family members, many of whom had died or been killed during the war.

In 1948, John moved to Toronto, where he continued his education and eventually became an accountant. John met and married his wife, Nora, there. They have three children and ten grandchildren. Today, John continues to speak in schools and libraries about his experiences during the Holocaust. The story of John's experiences in the Second World War can also be found in Kathy Kacer's *The Underground Reporters* (Second Story Press).

THE LIBERATION
OF DACHAU

• Dachau, 1945 •

ELLY GOTZ'S STORY—A FIVE-MINUTE PLAY

Elly, sixteen, Kovno Ghetto, 1944.

CAST OF CHARACTERS

ELLY, *seventeen years old; six feet, one inch tall; weighs seventy pounds*

PAPA, *fifty-four years old; six feet tall; weighs seventy to eighty pounds*

STRANGER #1

GERMAN SOLDIER

STRANGER #2

KAZET POLIZEI, *prisoners, supervised by the* kapos *(who were privileged prisoners themselves), who distributed food in the camps*

Scene 1

A train between Dachau #1 Camp and the Central (main) Dachau Camp.

(The train is packed with sick, emaciated men. A seventeen-year-old boy and his father crouch on the floor of the train. Father and son are mere skin and bones, and while the boy still has fight in him, the father's will is waning.)

ELLY

Papa, wake up.

PAPA

I am tired, Elly. Let me rest.

ELLY

We're almost there.

PAPA

A whole night it takes to travel a few kilometres? Stop, start, stop, start.

ELLY

The train is slowing down, Papa.

PAPA

Fast, slow, stop, go—what's the difference?

ELLY

No, this is different. Can you hear the echo? We are in a station, a shunting yard. Look through the cracks, Papa. It's a big railway yard. The train is stopping.

PAPA

The train has stopped a dozen times already.

ELLY

Listen to the brakes. We are stopping for good. Come, move around, Papa. Stretch.

PAPA

There is no room to stretch. There is no room to move!

STRANGER #1

Leave him alone. He's an old man.

ELLY

He's not old, and mind your own business.

STRANGER #1

It is my business. You are talking too much. And look at him—his legs are swollen and his skin has no colour.

ELLY

Shut up. And how can you tell the colour of his skin? It's too dark in here.

STRANGER #1

I can tell by his voice. He'll be dead by morning.

ELLY

No he won't. We lived a whole year in Dachau 1. And the war will soon be over. He'll make it. You'll see.

STRANGER #1

As you said, I can't see anything.

Scene 2

Railway line, early morning.

(*A train rumbles into a large rail yard filled with other parked trains. Cattle car doors open. Sunlight temporarily blinds the occupants. German soldiers are standing on the platform.*)

GERMAN SOLDIER

Schnell! Schnell! Off the train. Off the train.

PAPA

The smell, Elly—

ELLY

Never mind that. Just walk, Papa.

GERMAN SOLDIER

Schnell!

PAPA

It's the stench of death.

ELLY

It's the other trains. They are filled with dead bodies. We are in a station of some kind. Look, that train on the other track is riddled with bullets.

STRANGER #1

This whole place is filled with dead bodies.

GERMAN SOLDIER

Schnell!

ELLY

Here's your bowl. Don't lose the bowl. Keep walking, Papa.
Soon, soon the war will be over. The Allies will come.

GERMAN SOLDIER

(Overhearing and holding up his gun.)
The end of the war makes no difference to you, Jew. See this?
The last bullet is for you.

ELLY

Lean on me, Papa.

PAPA

I want to lie down, Elly. I just want to lie down.

GERMAN SOLDIER

March, march. To the left, to the left.

ELLY

Where are they making us go? The showers, they are sending
us to the showers.

PAPA

The Germans go to such effort to kill us. The war is almost
at an end and still they murder. We must be very important
to them, Elly.

ELLY

Look, I see people coming out the other side of the showers. They are putting on clean clothes.

PAPA

They are putting on cleaner rags.

ELLY

Walk faster, Papa, you are shuffling. I want a shower. I want to get rid of these lice.

Scene 3

Barracks, beds stacked four bunks high on either side.

PAPA

I must lie down.

ELLY

There must be hundreds of men packed in here.

PAPA

There, up there. I can lie down there.

ELLY

That's too high up. Come, we will find something else.

PAPA

There.

ELLY

But there is only room for one.

PAPA

Leave me here, Elly.

ELLY

No, we will stay together. You must not lie down, Papa. Please. You must keep moving. You must.

PAPA

(Crawls into second-level bunk.)
I am tired, Elly. Here, take my bowl and see if you can get soup. Go, Elly. Let me rest.

ELLY

Papa …

PAPA

Go, Elly. Leave me.

Scene 4

Food lineup. Open air.

(Stranger #2 stands behind Elly.)

STRANGER #2

You think they will give you two bowls of soup?

ELLY

I can ask.

STRANGER #2

They kill for asking. There is no way to tell how the *kapos* will behave. You should know that.

ELLY

My father is sick. See? You can see him from here. He is on the second bunk. Wave to him. He will wave back.

STRANGER #2

I see him. He will not last much longer.

ELLY

He will last. We only have each other. My mother—we don't know where she is. And my aunt and uncles—gone. He will live. He promised me. He will not leave me alone.

STRANGER #2

You think it is his choice that he lives or dies?

ELLY

"Choose life," that is what Moses said.

STRANGER #2

Moses was a Jew. Jesus was a Jew. These Nazis would kill their own Saviour. What chance do we have?

ELLY

My father will live. The war will soon be over. Perhaps the Americans will come.

STRANGER #2

The Americans have been coming for years. Do you see any Americans? Do you hear any Americans?

ELLY

They are coming. I know they are coming.

KAZET POLIZEI

Two bowls? You don't get two bowls of soup.

ELLY

Please. One is for my father. See, he is over there. He is waving.

KAZET POLIZEI

Next time, he comes and gets his own soup and bread.

STRANGER #2

(Walking away with Elly.)

He gave you two soups and two breads? No Kazet Polizei or *kapos* behave this way. You are right—the war is ending. But they will kill us first, you'll see.

A roar is heard in the distance. An American tank breaks down the main gate and comes to a stop. Jeeps follow, and American soldiers march in on foot. Everyone stops and looks at each other. Elly runs to his father.

ELLY

They are here, Papa. They are here. We are free. We made it, Papa. We are free. Papa, wake up! PAPA! What's wrong with you? Wake up. Open your eyes. Not now, Papa, don't die now! The Americans are here, right here!

PAPA

(Opens eyes slowly.)

That is good—but did you bring the bread?

POSTSCRIPT

Elly and his father survived the Holocaust and survived what was to come next. Overwhelmed by the thousands of bodies that lay in heaps, by the emaciated walking skeletons that greeted them, the Americans doled out cans of beef. Now unused to solid food, many inmates developed diarrhea (dubbed "The Last Run") and died as the Americans looked on helplessly.

With the help of the Red Cross and other support agencies, Elly's mother and aunt were found alive, along with three uncles.

The Gotz family eventually moved from Europe to Rhodesia (later called Zimbabwe), and finally to Canada in 1964. Elly and his wife, Esme, have three children and six grandchildren.

"THE OPPRESSED FREED THE PERSECUTED"

• Ebensee (a sub-camp of Mauthausen Camp), 1945 •

MAX (TIBOR) EISEN'S STORY

Max, right, at about nine years old, with his brothers, Eugene, six,
and Alfred, two, in Moldava, Czechloslovakia, 1938.

May 6, 1945

There was a commotion outside of his barrack, a sort of hum in the air. And something else besides—a rumble in the distance, like thunder crawling across an open sky. It took two tries before Max could sit up. Knees, elbows—all his joints stuck out like knotted ropes under reptilian skin. As he moved, bone grated against bone and his teeth wobbled in his gums. Even the cartilage in his ears and his nose had dissolved. Then there was the typhus, which had left him half-mad with fever.

He stood and steadied himself. Walking quickly was out of the question; even putting one foot in front of the other took more energy than he had to spare. Slowly, carefully, as if one wrong move would send his body crashing to the ground, he stumbled outside. The boy was sixteen years old, yet he lurched about like a very old man. He stood on the threshold of his barrack and looked out onto the parade grounds. Something was different, but what? He was in Ebensee, one of the sixty sub-camps of the Mauthausen concentration camp. The camp was in Austria, near the town of Linz, Adolf Hitler's hometown. He had been in many camps: Auschwitz, Melk, and now this one.

There was an odd rumble under his feet. He looked up at the guard towers. They were empty. He looked again, and again. The SS guards, with their death-head insignia, were no longer in the towers. No guards! Look, look, the flagpole! A white flag flew! His heart began to thump hard. It was wonderful … too wonderful. But wait. Maybe it was a mistake. Maybe it was a trick. The typhus had turned his mind into a jumble of disconnected thoughts. It was hard to think straight, harder still to process information. Over and over he was told, they were all told, "Who wins the war is no concern of yours. No Jew will be left alive." But there were no guards, a white flag flew, and here he was, alive!

The ground vibrated as the rumble under his feet became a roar. Something was just beyond the gate, something large. There was a thunderous crash as a tank smashed through the gates of Ebensee.

"Americans." The word was whispered from man to man. And then the American tank rolled right into the middle of the camp and stopped.

Was it a delusion? The boy shuffled towards the tank, his hands outstretched. If he could feel the metal, then maybe he could make it real.

Now walking skeletons emerged from the gloom of the buildings. Zombie-like, they stumbled forward with startled, vacant eyes.

American soldiers sat on the turret of the tank, guns primed and ready to face the enemy, to fight the good fight. What hell had they stumbled into? A soldier sitting high up on the tank, his helmet low over his eyes, hissed into his radio, "Sergeant, you better get up here. No … no … you have to see this."

More skeletons emerged from the buildings, more and more, until they surrounded the tank. Spidery fingers reached up to touch their liberators. Horrified, the soldiers tried to scramble farther up the tank.

"Mother of God, look!" What a young soldier had thought was a pile of sticks could now be seen to be skulls, rib cages, hands, and feet. Corpses were stacked up like cordwood. He let out a slow, deep wail.

The stench of decomposed bodies hung over the camp like a dense fog, suffocating and stifling. One soldier, then another, and another, and another bent double at the waist and vomited. Occasionally someone yelled a command, but mostly there was silence.

"I think I know what this place is," whispered one soldier to another. "It's one of those Nazi camps. Concentration camps, that's what they're called. I heard about them somewhere."

"You American?" The boy's voice gurgled up his windpipe. He hadn't used it in a long time. These Americans had black skin. He had never seen a black man, not up close, not in person. Their black skin looked beautiful, shiny and healthy. His own skin continually shed great flakes and was blanched, like bones left too long under a desert sun.

The black American soldier nodded, too overwhelmed to speak. At home, in the United States, signs hung outside of stores: "No Dogs, No Negroes." Blacks were not even allowed to fight alongside white soldiers. Racism thrived, particularly in the southern states. The blacks in America were oppressed, but this? What was this?

There was a sudden flurry of activity as soldiers leapt about trying to find something, anything, to ease the pain of the dying people around them. Pots of soup were set up and a line began to form. The boy watched the scene unfold around him.

His name was Max Eisen, son of Zoltan and Ethel Friedman Eisen, brother to Eugene, Alfred, and baby sister Judith, all dead. His whole family gone.

They had almost made it. The Eisens' home was in the little corner of Czechoslovakia that was handed to Hungary, and Hungary was not taken over by the Nazis until March 1944. They had thought that maybe, just maybe, they had missed it all. After all, it was rumoured that the Germans were losing the war. Maybe they were safe.

But then, after Passover of that same year, the police and the Nazis had pounded down the door of their home. Within moments the Eisen family had been robbed, ousted, and, along with four hundred other Jewish families, paraded through town. Max, just fifteen years old, had walked beside his father, his mother, his grandparents, his brothers, and whispered, "Father, what will happen to our dogs?"

As Max stood in the camp, as he touched the hard metal of the tanks and watched the Americans pass out blankets, he remembered his parents, his relatives, his dogs.

The smell of the broth mingled with the stench of decay. Max sat and waited. Never again would he line up for food. The war was over. The Holocaust had come to an end.

Max whispered, "What was it all about?"

POSTSCRIPT

The 761st Tank Battalion unit was made up of highly trained black soldiers. U.S. federal law did not allow black soldiers to serve with white troops. The motto of the 761st was "Come Out Fighting." They suffered a great deal of racism, hence the phrase, coined after the liberation of the Ebensee concentration camp, "the oppressed freed the persecuted."

Max Eisen was the only survivor of his immediate family. Of the seventy-three members of his extended family, only two cousins survived. He did return to his village of Szepsi, now called Moldava, in Czechoslovakia. A neighbour who had taken over their home and family farm recognized Max immediately. When Max asked her for a glass of milk, she refused.

Today, Max lives in Toronto with his wife, Ivy Cosman. They have two sons, Edmund and Larry, two grand-daughters, Amy and Julie, and one great-granddaughter, Judith. Retired, Max has passed his business to his sons. Sailing, canoeing, and gardening are his passions.

GLOSSARY

Adolf Hitler Born in 1889, Hitler came to power in 1933 when he was elected Chancellor of Germany. Hitler promised to restore prosperity to the German people following their economic devastation in the First World War. Under his leadership, Germany invaded Poland in September 1939 to begin the Second World War. His racial policies culminated in the killing of more than six million Jews and more than five million other people. He committed suicide in the final days of the war in 1945.

Allies The countries that joined forces in an alliance to oppose what were known as the Axis powers (see Axis powers). The Allies included the United States, Great Britain, the Soviet Union—known as "the big three"— Canada, France, South Africa, and many others.

Auschwitz The largest of the concentration camps, it was named after the town of Oswiecim, located close by in Poland. There were actually three main camps in Auschwitz: Auschwitz I (the administrative camp), Auschwitz II (or Birkenau, the death camp), and

Auschwitz III (a labour camp). There were also approximately forty smaller camps surrounding Auschwitz. It is estimated that of the six million Jews who were killed in the Holocaust, at least 1.6 million perished in Auschwitz.

Axis powers The three major countries opposed to the Allies were Germany, Italy, and Japan. The term "axis" came from Benito Mussolini, the Prime Minister of Italy during the Second World War. He said that Germany and Italy would form an "axis," and other countries in Europe would revolve around this partnership.

Belzec One of the death camps located in Poland. It is estimated that more than 400,000 Jews were killed there along with an unknown number of Poles and Roma people.

Birkenau Part of the Auschwitz concentration camp, Birkenau was established in 1941 as a death camp. It was the location of the gas chambers of Auschwitz and was also called Auschwitz II. Of the main camps, Birkenau had the largest prisoner population.

Blechhammer A British prisoner-of-war camp, located in Poland.

Block The buildings or barracks that held the Jewish prisoners in the concentration camps. These were long, wooden structures that were built to house approximately 250 prisoners, but often housed over 1000 people. Inside these blocks, there were three tiers of wooden platforms where the inmates slept. The buildings were unheated in the winter, and provided little or no protection from the elements.

Boxcar Jews were transported to concentration camps in railway boxcars that had previously been used to transport freight and/or cattle. Hundreds of Jews could be jammed into a small space and transported for days before reaching their destination. Many Jews died on the trip to the concentration camps.

Chelmno One of the death camps located in Germany. It is estimated that at least 150,000 Jews were killed there.

Concentration camps The prison camps, death camps, and labour camps where Jews and other people were sent. Hitler established more than one hundred major concentration camps and several thousand smaller camps.

Dachau The first of the concentration camps that was opened in Germany in 1933. Over 200,000 people were imprisoned there. Two-thirds of those were political prisoners, and one-third were Jewish prisoners. Dachau was liberated by the American forces in 1945. It was one of the first opportunities for those in the West to witness the brutality that had taken place in these camps over the course of the war.

Death camps Also called "extermination camps," the major ones were Treblinka, Auschwitz-Birkenau, Dachau, Chelmno, Sobibor, Belzec, and Majdanek. These death camps were established as part of Hitler's "Final Solution for the Jewish Question," his plan to systematically kill the Jews of Europe. The primary method for killing was the gas chamber, large warehouse buildings into which Jews were herded. The doors were then locked and gas (Zyklon B) was dispersed, killing all those inside.

Death march Towards the end of 1944, the Nazis decided to abandon the concentration camps, moving or destroying evidence of the crimes they had committed. Tens of thousands of Jewish prisoners were marched for days at a time, without food or shelter. This march became known as the "death march." The prisoners were being marched to other concentration camps deep inside Germany. Ultimately, the Nazis hoped to reduce the ranks of the living and then load those still alive onto boats at the Baltic Sea and sink the ships.

Debrecen The second largest city in Hungary, it was almost completely destroyed during the Second World War.

Displaced Persons Camps These were temporary facilities established after the war to house Jews who had been uprooted from their homes. Millions of survivors had nowhere to go when the war ended. DP camps were built in Germany, France, Italy, and Belgium, often on or close to the sites of previous concentration camps.

Ebensee One of the sub-camps of the Mauthausen concentration camp, located in Austria. Its purpose was to provide slave labour for the construction of underground tunnels in which rockets and other Nazi armaments were being stored. Thousands died from the gruelling work conditions and thousands of others were sent to the gas chambers of Mauthausen.

Flossenburg Established in 1938, this prison camp was located in Germany near the border with Czechoslovakia. Originally, Jews and criminals were imprisoned there. Eventually it grew to include political and foreign prisoners of war as well. There was a large stone quarry nearby where prisoners were put to work. More than 30,000 prisoners died there.

Gas chamber A sealed building into which gas was introduced (mainly Zyklon B) for the purpose of killing those inside. During the Holocaust, large-scale gas chambers were designed for mass killings. Typically, the gas chamber had three components: an area to undress, a large gas chamber where the killing took place, and a crematorium oven where the bodies of those killed were burned. In some cases, bodies were buried in mass graves.

Gestapo The short term for *Geheime Staatspolizei*, or the Secret State Police of Germany. The force was established in 1933. Under Hitler, the Gestapo had the power to operate in whatever way they wished. They could arrest, confine, and interrogate anyone who was thought to oppose Germany's political position. They also were responsible for setting up and administering the concentration camps.

Ghetto The enclosed area of a city or town that separated Jews from the rest of the community. Between 1939 and 1945, Hitler established 356 ghettos in Poland, the Soviet Union, the Baltic states, Czechoslovakia, Romania, and Hungary.

Gleiwitz A sub-camp of the Auschwitz concentration camp. It had a large facility where Jewish prisoners were put to work repairing railway cars.

Gross-Rosen Originally a satellite camp to Sachsenhausen, this concentration camp became independent on May 1, 1941. It was known for its brutal treatment of prisoners in its enormous stone quarry. More than 40,000 inmates perished there.

Holocaust The word means "a burnt or sacrificial offering," and it is the term given to the Nazi genocide or systematic killing of more than six million Jews during the Second World War.

Iron Guard The political party and army of Romania during the Second World War. Founded by Corneliu Zelea Codreanu, the Iron Guard was extremely anti-Semitic and participated actively in the eradication of Jews throughout eastern Romania.

Josef Mengele The concentration camp doctor in Auschwitz, he was known as "the Angel of Death." Mengele was in charge of the selections. He also masterminded a series of scientific experiments using Jewish prisoners as subjects. Most of his victims died in these human experiments. He escaped to Argentina at the end of the war, and died in an accidental drowning in Brazil in 1979.

Judenfrei A German word used to designate areas as "free of Jews."

Kapo Prisoners in the concentration camps who worked for the Nazi guards and carried out their orders. In exchange for this, they received more food and better living conditions.

Kazet Polizei Prisoners, supervised by the *kapos* (who were privileged prisoners themselves), who distributed food in the camps.

Laufer A German word for "runner." Young boys were put to work in the concentration camps as messenger boys, doing odd jobs for the camp commanders. This was a desirable position that brought with it extra rations and other privileges.

Majdanek One of the death camps located close to the Polish town of Lublin. It was established in October 1941. At least 100,000 Jews were killed there in the gas chambers. It was ultimately liberated by the Soviet Red Army.

Nazi The short form for *Nationalsozialistische Deutsche Arbeiterpartei*, or the National Socialist German Workers Party. This was the political party of Adolf Hitler.

Obersturmbannführer A senior military rank of the Nazi Party.

Obersturmführer A junior military rank of the Nazi Party.

Rosh Hashanah The Jewish New Year. One of the holiest days in the Jewish religion, it is a day of prayer and repentance.

Ravensbruck Opened in 1939 and located in Germany, north of Berlin, it was the only major concentration camp for women. In 1941, a small men's camp was opened close by. Of the approximately 130,000 female prisoners in Ravensbruck between 1939 and 1945, only about 40,000 survived.

Selection Jews arriving in the death camps were subject to a selection. Prisoners were lined up and had to pass in front of an SS officer who inspected them. Those who looked strong and were fit to work were separated from those destined for the gas chambers.

Shabbat The Jewish Sabbath, celebrated from sundown Friday until sundown Saturday.

Shofar A ram's horn that is blown like a trumpet on Rosh Hashanah.

Sobibor One of the death camps located in Poland. As many as 200,000 people were killed here. The camp was closed in 1943 following the escape of approximately 300 prisoners.

Sonderkommando A special unit of Jewish prisoners who were forced to help with the killing process in the death camps. They would accompany Jews to the gas chambers, remove their bodies from the gas chambers, and dispose of them. They were not allowed any contact with other prisoners lest they give out any information about what was happening.

SS An acronym for the German word *Schutzstaffel* or "protection squad." This force was created in 1925 to be Hitler's bodyguards and later became the elite unit of the Nazi Party. Members of the SS staffed the concentration camps, the police, and the military.

Transnistria A Ukrainian territory acquired by Germany in 1941, and put under Romanian administration.

Treblinka One of the death camps established in 1942 in Poland. It is estimated that almost 800,000 people were killed there.

Yom Kippur Considered the holiest and most solemn of the Jewish holidays, this is a day of fasting, praying, and asking forgiveness for the sins of the past year. It is also called the Day of Atonement.

ACKNOWLEDGMENTS

We are greatly indebted to the survivors and their families whose stories we have documented here: Felicia Steigman Carmelly, Bob Kornhauser, Judy Weissenberg Cohen, Fanny Frydman Pillerdorf, Arthur Kacer, Hellmuth Szprycer, Arnold Friedman, George Scott, George Brady, John Freund, Elly Gotz, and Max Eisen. Thank you for continuing to talk about your life histories, so that your stories will continue to be heard. We are in awe of your courage and heroism.

Thanks as always to the hard-working team at Penguin Group (Canada): Jennifer Notman, Catherine Marjoribanks, Eleanor Gasparik, David Ross, and Lisa Lapointe. We are grateful for your commitment and dedication to this series.

To our families and friends who guide, encourage, and support us, we return the love.